The Bleed of Heaven

The Bleed of Heaven

Or Luke and Me

Kris Brown

RESOURCE *Publications* • Eugene, Oregon

THE BLEED OF HEAVEN
Or Luke and Me

Copyright © 2021 Kris Brown. All rights reserved. Except for brief quotations in critical publications or reviews, no part of this book may be reproduced in any manner without prior written permission from the publisher. Write: Permissions, Wipf and Stock Publishers, 199 W. 8th Ave., Suite 3, Eugene, OR 97401.

Resource Publications
An Imprint of Wipf and Stock Publishers
199 W. 8th Ave., Suite 3
Eugene, OR 97401

www.wipfandstock.com

PAPERBACK ISBN: 978-1-7252-8811-9
HARDCOVER ISBN: 978-1-7252-8812-6
EBOOK ISBN: 978-1-7252-8813-3

05/17/21

Scripture quotations from the New Revised Standard Version Bible, New International Version Bible, and the King James Bible appear in this text.

Scriptures taken from the New Revised Standard Version Bible, copyright © 1989 National Council of the Churches of Christ in the United States of America. Used by permission. All rights reserved worldwide.

Scriptures taken from the Holy Bible, New International Version®, NIV®. Copyright © 1973, 1978, 1984, 2011 by Biblica, Inc.™ Used by permission of Zondervan. All rights reserved worldwide. www.zondervan.com The "NIV" and "New International Version" are trademarks registered in the United States Patent and Trademark Office by Biblica, Inc.®

Scriptures taken from The Authorized (King James) Version. Rights in the Authorized Version in the United Kingdom are vested in the Crown. Reproduced by permission of the Crown's patentee, Cambridge University Press.

A part of what follows began as an article published in Brill's *Horizons in Biblical Theology*, Volume 38, Issue 1 in 2016.

Contents

Acknowledgments | vii

Beginnings: Where Is God in This? | 1

The Gospel

| I | The Joy and Peril of Reading Greek | 9
| II | New Wine Into New Wineskins | 12
| III | An Early Christmas | 17
| IV | Coming Into Being | 20
| V | Becoming | 21
| VI | Not Whatever | 28
| VII | Piling Up Things | 31
| VIII | Collapse | 35
| IX | Locating Hope | 40
| X | Breaking Us Open | 47
| XI | My Dad And Me | 49
| XII | Taking In Forgiveness | 54
| XIII | Heading Toward Jerusalem | 62
| XIV | Defeat | 65
| XV | Crucifixion and All That Will Not Hold Together | 69

How Acts Means

| XVI | Wittgenstein and My Grandmother | 77
| XVII | Shipwreck | 81

XVIII	How Things Are In Acts	83
IXX	Horse Stories	88
XX	The Slipperiness Of Meaning	93
XXI	Alex Krutov	96
XXII	The Blessings We Need	101
XXIII	The Hole In The Middle	108
XXIV	Philip and the Eunuch	110
XXV	The Floor Drops Out	113
XXVI	Piecing Things Together	116
XXVII	Turning Around	118
XXVIII	A God Who Lifts Up	124
XXIX	What Does This Thing Wish To Be?	130
XXX	What Acts Acts Out	131
XXXI	An Easter Story	135

Acknowledgments

THANKS TO MY ENCOURAGING friends and early readers, especially to Jean, Christine, and Melissa. Thanks to my brilliant teacher, Lewie, who very much made this project possible and who has opened wide the faith of so many. Thanks, of course, to David, Henry, and Alex, along with our dear animal family, for their love and support as well as for continually making all things new.

SOME OF MY STORIES necessarily involve the stories of others. None of us is finished. Thank God, God can be trusted to hold all our stories even though we are barely able to see who is in front of us.

Beginnings

Where Is God in This?

For most of my life, I have been on the fence about God. I am not quite able to think that evolutionary history, the thousands of stars you begin to notice after you have found the Big Dipper, the ridiculously perfect interplay of animals and plants, carbon dioxide to oxygen to carbon dioxide to oxygen, the stream of human consciousness, and the stream of my thoughts have come out of nothing. But whatever it is moving forward and backward and sideways through experience and time, what can we make of it? The queen ant sometimes sacrifices her colony to hold onto her place, then there is that anteater, and then someone to eat him. Lines that lead to nowhere. Greed. Betrayal. Loss. Tragedy. My own. Yours. What we know.

Not the "God is good" stuff you might hear in a church, if you were to go in. Maybe after a nice piece of coconut cake with a fruited tea, or while looking up and noticing the sparkle jumping out of a crystal sky framing the deepest green pine right in front of you that smells like Christmas, maybe then you or I might whisper something like, "You know, God isn't so bad." But what exactly are we saying? Under what conditions do we accept God? Under what conditions does God accept us? And how will we know whether or not the two of us are getting along?

How do we go about answering such questions? What is. What God must be. What God must be because of what is. What God must be in spite of what is. Hamster-wheeling, I tend, when faced with something I don't understand, to head to school. If I

The Bleed of Heaven

were in the right room with a white board across the back wall, I would start with a big Roman numeral I. And write something down. Then maybe a I.a. Even a I.a.1, then a I.a.2. "God is . . ." Maybe you would agree with whatever it is I wrote. And we would go out of the room thinking that we had accomplished something. No doubt, we would have accomplished something. But of course, once we were outside, a slap in the face, an illness, the wrong pair of shoes, would start working against what we had come up with.

What might I never have thought?

And how do I (or you) get to such a place?

Raised a Jew, I can't help remembering all that Old Testament wandering. Being lost, coming to the Promised Land, being there, being thrown out, and then trying again. Judaism (along with Christianity and Islam) begins when wandering Abraham walks out into the desert and drags his clan along with him. We read Abraham's main story about his willingness to obey God even to the point of sacrificing his son, and we are supposed to say to ourselves something like, "God does interact with us. Thank God." But that story. What kind of God is that? "Abraham, take your son on a trip, then at the end of it, kill him." We know the whole business eventually works out, but what happens to Isaac, to Abraham on that journey? As Isaac is being bound? What is the lesson?

How do we read God stories and find God in them? So many of these stories force you down on your knees. Abraham is a good man because he believes God even to the point of tying up his son. But when my own head is down, my body prostrate, I can't help it. I say to myself, "This isn't fair." Maybe you do too? And then we sit, quiet because we are dazed, defeated, on the fence, wondering about where we are, watching the stars come up, group by group, in the night sky.

Abraham, in fact, is a huge problem. Because I was thinking about him, I re-read his story. No matter what sort of wiggling you do, you wouldn't want to be a member of his family. The sacrificing Isaac stuff begins "after these things." After trickery and jealousy and foolishness. After Abraham got rid of his other son along with Ishmael's mother by sending them both out into the desert. After

Beginnings

these things, Abraham forces his remaining son to walk and walk and walk with him and pick up the wood for his own death fire. Somehow, we feel that we are supposed to pay close attention to how hard all this is on Abraham. Abraham is willing to sacrifice his own son to prove his faith. God approves. Abraham is okay.

We believe that Abraham's story teaches us what God wants. God comes up with a test. Abraham passes. Once Isaac is tied up, ready to go, God finds out what God needs to know about Abraham. Yet, if this is the situation, then God is also being tested. What does God learn? What would God think if Abraham didn't bind Isaac? Why does Abraham matter so much to God?

I want a different story. I find myself almost arguing out loud as I read. "Look God, this man has involved his family in unspeakable misery, misery that will become mythic, that will tear peoples apart for centuries, tears them apart right now. Get Ishmael out of the desert. Fix it." But how do you fix "after these things," after you and I have done this and then done that? And if you could snap your fingers and straighten things out, what would happen to the person you were following behind, cleaning up after? What would you feel about that person? What would he or she do next? What would he or she feel about you?

I suppose it's a bit of a stretch to imagine oneself in God's shoes. It is not much easier to think about Abraham. What exactly does Abraham learn because of his trip with Isaac? He doesn't let us know. But in the middle of what seems to be pointless cruelty supposedly illustrating the value of loyalty, the ground shifts. Abraham hears the voice of God say, "Do not lay a hand on that boy. Do not do anything to him." A clear message. I hope Isaac hears that voice too; I hope he knows God is on his side. And I hope Abraham thinks about Ishmael as he unbinds Isaac. Maybe it takes the trip and the firewood and the binding for Abraham to sort out what he has done.

How do you face yourself when you are untying one son, the other son lost in the desert? Brittle in your own goodness, overlooking what you have done, opining, thinking about moving on.

The Bleed of Heaven

What sort of God do you see? I myself tend to go back to my fence, looking for a way out, one that is not too difficult.

As I am sitting up there, I like to read. Maybe as an escape (by the time I die, I am certain to have set some sort of re-reading Jane Austen record). But too often words on a page don't work the way I want them to. Even Jane Austen begins to mess with you. I come inside *Pride and Prejudice* or *Emma* and find myself slightly unsettled, implicated. I read on. I can't help myself.

Reading myself in and out, I begin to connect, dot-to-dot. Usually, the trail I make becomes a picture I wasn't expecting. I don't always see the picture at first; I don't always understand what I am reading or why what I find myself almost compelled to finish matters so much. I don't exactly remember when I started to experience reading the bible like this. Maybe most of us, if we read around in the bible for very long, especially if we are reading from the gospels, feel at least the beginnings of a peculiar kind of pressure. We sit perplexed, or at least I do, and say to ourselves something like, "This is not the God I have imagined. What am I going to do with this? What is going to happen (to me) next?"

What *am* I going to do with this? After I tried to describe to a skeptical friend what it was that I was trying to write, she asked me, "But who would read such a thing?" Hmmm. All I could manage as an answer was a sort-of list of what I did not intend, but oddly, my list pulled together for me a reader I might not at first have recognized. Someone who, like me, wanted to see God in her (or his) life, but had a great deal of trouble doing so, but continued to ask anyway, "What is God doing? Where is God?" And so forth.

Surely we all, at least at times, hope to see the trace of God in our lives. Maybe for a few of us the outlines are obvious. I guess I am writing for and to everyone else. When I sit with the bible open, funny things begin to happen. Funny things that have led me to Greek, to Hebrew (not yet an altogether productive journey), and around the block. There and back again. Sometimes when I return, I feel that I have barely gotten out alive. Luke especially does this to me. Carefully interviewing, recalling, collecting this person, then that person, story after story, Luke seems friendly enough as he

Beginnings

invites us into his gospel then Acts. But seconds after we sit down at the table, we find we are sweating, squirming in our seats.

Yet, if Luke were here talking with me, before long, I imagine I would be telling him my stories. You might too. We, Luke and me (and you?), would begin again and again, comparing notes, following what we have heard just a little farther, starting one trip then another, perhaps, after enough time had passed, feeling like we were, haltingly, getting somewhere.

With Luke along, we couldn't help but get somewhere. Reading Luke involves jumping off the fence, seeing for the first time clearly a meadow with flowers, maybe a pond, a few jackrabbits, and huge round hay bales on the other side, coming to an open gate, going through, finding yourself in that pasture at night, with stars and stars, even shooting stars, overhead, then you see some shepherds in the corner. You walk toward them thinking that you will talk with them and maybe then just go back and climb up into the hay. But . . .

The Gospel

The Gospel

— I —

The Joy and Peril of Reading Greek

WILL THOSE SHEPHERDS LEAVE me behind? And how will I hear them, each in their own voice, hear any of the many, many voices from so, so long ago? How to hear Luke himself, words on a page, but words also from an ancient writer to a friend?

When I am talking with someone I don't understand, I don't know what else to do, but to slow down. Sitting with Luke next to me, I fiddle, word by word, with Greek. Maybe at first because I want to imagine that Luke's language brings me closer to whatever it was that happened or was said or was pointed to, but pretty quickly because reading Greek, even just a few lines in a couple of manuscripts or groups of manuscripts, so often invites me into something very much like conversation, the best kind of conversation where you puzzle together something that suddenly wakes you up and makes you want to know more.

Skip what follows if it looks too strange on the page. I don't know how else to share the experience, but to sort of dive in. So that looking over *"hoi de eipan pros auton, hoi mathatai . . ."* (It doesn't really help to transcribe Greek into English, does it? But you get the idea.), I try to translate each word: "*But/and they said to him, [on account of why] the disciples of John fast often and make prayers and also those of the Pharisees, but yours eat and drink[?].*"

Almost immediately, things go wrong. A couple of manuscripts add the *"on account of why,"* so that sometimes this sentence is a question. A question is so much softer than a declaration.

The Gospel

Exactly how rude are these people talking with Jesus? What is their intention? I like the question better. Without it, "they," whoever is talking, seem more obnoxious, but I think either way the sentence means the same thing. Or does it? Now I have to read on.

Jesus answers the ruder non-questioners with a question: *"But/ and Jesus said to them, 'Are you able* (grammar means the answer is no) *to make the sons of the bridal hall, while the bridegroom is with them, to fast?'"* Or, to the less rude crowd in the other manuscripts, the ones who ask a question rather than spout off what they think is obvious, Jesus just makes a statement: *"The sons of the wedding hall are not able to fast while the bridegroom is with them."* The two versions sort of balance out, but who is doing the balancing?

And why? Suddenly, I am hearing the voices of much later manuscript writers (who exactly are they?). Maybe even watching a few of them make mistakes. So that next, among manuscripts, there is a floating *"kai"* (*"and,"* but sometimes *"even," "also"*). Yet surely, this is the sentence: *"But the days will come, when the bridegroom is taken away/lifted up/removed from them and then they will fast in those days."* Getting to the end, things sort of fall together on the page. Fasting yes. But fasting is not what we thought it was. Fasting as grief, not fasting as show.

Okay. It feels like Jesus and Luke are moving to some kind of summary: *"And/but he was saying a parable to them that . . ."* Jesus's "parable" will expand upon fasting as grief being good but fasting as show being bad. But no. Jesus's "parable" involves some pretty complicated Greek that doesn't seem to be about grief or show or even fasting: *"No one, having torn from a new garment a patch throws it upon an old garment. If not otherwise* (nice idiom) *also/ and/even the new will split and with the old will not be compatible, even the old patch, the one from the new."* Jesus's answer to a question about fasting changes the nature of the question. Somehow, the question becomes about old and new practice.

Then Luke's Jesus doubles down: *"And no one puts new wine into old wineskins, if not otherwise* (same idiom linking this to sentence which comes right before) *the wine breaks apart the wineskin, and it will be poured out, and the wineskin will be destroyed."*

The Joy and Peril of Reading Greek

Ripped garments, destroyed wineskin; seems like things are getting worse. I think destroyed wineskins are in worse shape than ripped garments? Old and new cannot be together. How hard is this becoming? What exactly is Jesus talking about?

"*But new wine into new wineskins must be put.*" One manuscript is so uncomfortable that it adds to the end, "*and both are kept safe.*" Should both be kept safe? Most manuscripts are silent, don't add anything about safety. What to do with the old/ new split? We come to the end or at least a break: *"And no one drinking old desires new, for he says the old is of a quality/suitable/pleasant."* Should we like these folks drinking the old? Where are we here? One manuscript adds *"immediately"*: *"And no one drinking old immediately wishes new."* A word to push for the possibility of change. Maybe the old wine drinkers will come around eventually?

— II —

New Wine Into New Wineskins

And they said to him, "The disciples of John often fast and make prayers, likewise the ones of the Pharisees, but yours eat and drink." And Jesus said to them, "Are you able to make the sons of the wedding hall fast when the bridegroom is with them? But the days will come also when the bridegroom is taken away from them, then they will fast in those days." And he was also saying a parable to them that no one, having torn [it], puts a patch from a new garment on an old garment. The new will split, and the patch will not match the old with the new. And no one throws new wine into old wineskins. The new wine will burst the wineskins and itself will be poured out, and the wineskins will be destroyed. But new wine must be put into new wineskins. And no one having drunk the old wishes for new, for he says, "the old is good."

LUKE 5:33-39

THINGS FALL APART IN Luke. Events bleed into the stories that surround them. Then stories, parables, questions, if we let them, recast what we have just read. Pharisees and their scribes may come to Jesus and assert with confidence, "The disciples of John often fast and make prayers, likewise the ones of the Pharisees, but yours eat and drink." We hear Jesus respond to the Pharisees with what seems like a simple question. And next (then next, then next) a sequence happens, each moment naturally, even logically following what comes before, taking Jesus's hearers and, along with them, those of us reading, to unrecognizable, even dangerous places.

Reading in Luke, at least for me, often means re-reading. The whole process begins with a sort-of "huh?", then I realize I am in over my head. If you and I were to re-read the short passage above (and maybe even re-read it again), we might begin to hear the Pharisees' underlying snark, "What are you going to do about this, Jesus?" or "Who do you think you are, anyway?" For a moment, we might feel satisfied, like we'd solved a riddle. Good readers, we recognize the Pharisees' motives and intentions: the Pharisees are the bad guys. We might think we were finished.

And yet, if we continued to look back over our shoulders, we might wonder along with the crowd gathered around and following Jesus. If we were watching all that eating and drinking, what would we do with it? Especially if everyone around us had always told us how important fasting was. Especially if we ourselves had fasted more than once. Like the Pharisees, we might ask a nasty, but somehow also reasonable question. Who is Jesus anyway?

And what does Jesus have to do with us, with me? As what is unfolding around us begins to get under our skin, the second question, for me anyway, seems to follow from the first. The business about fasting or eating, about celebrating or not, hinges upon how we understand what we do when we act out our faiths. How should I, how should you "practice" religion? The answer seems easy. No doubt, in some recognizable way so that we and everyone else will know that we are doing it. It makes sense that we would want our attempts at connecting to God to make sense. That we would want to get a handle on them. Of course, we want to go on with our lives, doing this, being recognized for the difficulty of that; all the time, confident of the rules and of the meaning we make for ourselves.

The Gospel

Jesus response to the Pharisees is quiet, innocuous enough, on the face of it: "Are you able to make the sons of the wedding hall fast when the bridegroom is with them?" The answer is obviously "no." But answering Jesus slows us down, makes us squirm a little. "No" is not the end of it. We thought we were talking with Jesus about how we act when we are being religious. But somehow Jesus directs us instead to something we cannot do. Trying to reply, we might first ask ourselves whether we are able to make anyone do anything. Or we might start counting who it is that makes us so happy that, with them, we cannot be our normal appropriate selves. We might find ourselves fading out of our own pictures. There is that bridegroom . . . Once Jesus speaks, none of us who hear him is where we thought we were. Duty, strenuous activity, ritualistic sacrifice, all the stuff of our religious practice misses the point.

Religious discipleship, religious observance, turns out to be, in Jesus's presence, closer to a wedding party than it is to anything else. Before any of us listening have a chance to catch our breath, Jesus pushes forward. As he does so, the ground underneath our feet begins to rumble. Jesus tells us the party will end. At that time, his disciples will behave like the Pharisees want them to behave, but their fasting and praying will have little to do with planned, upright religious behavior. Without the bridegroom, they will be grieving. And in case we have missed the point, Jesus follows immediately with a parable that attempts to pry apart our overstrained fingers clutching to the sides of what we have practiced for so long. New wine bursts old wineskins. No patchwork job of holding onto the old in order to try to contain the new will do.

We work our way through Luke's sequence, and as we do so, we begin to wriggle. We think we have things figured out. With fake politeness, we are able, indirectly, to murmur, "Who do you think you are, Jesus?" But then we receive Jesus's puzzling answer, "I am the bridegroom." We feel a challenge in the air. "Do you (Pharisees and scribes) have any idea where you are? The new will burst through the old." Then another challenge: some (who are to be pitied? considered stupid? rejected? invited to keep drinking

New Wine Into New Wineskins

the new wine until they begin to taste its worth?) will want to hang onto the old.

If we look about ourselves, we find this sort of displacement ricocheting around Luke's landscape. The wineskin conversation happens inside Levi the tax collector's house. He is hosting a banquet for Jesus (he is celebrating with the bridegroom); at the same time, he is in the process of losing most of what he knows. Because of his encounter with Jesus, his tax collecting gig is either coming to an end or will be so radically different that he soon most likely will not be able to afford such banquets. Traditionally, we believe this Levi to be Matthew, the gospel writer. If he is, what has the new wine done to him? What is the sequence that ends in Matthew's gospel? Jesus leaves the banquet, and we next find him plucking the heads of grain on a Sabbath. New wine again. Wine that reaches back to David and forward to the healing Jesus is about to perform. And threatens some who want to hold onto the old.

We cannot make a move in Luke without being subject to this sort of ricochet. We may try to explain what happens to us as we read in terms of thematic repetitions, the new bursting through the old, the low being lifted, the high being brought down. Certainly, such themes repeat in Luke. Yet Luke's gospel is not a flat land where themes pile up on top of themselves. Instead, Luke structures his gospel around the ricochet, and, at the same time, his profound distrust of structure makes our reading more and more urgent; we feel we are chasing an ever-moving target and that the landscape is blowing up behind us.

In the midst of all this movement, we hear again and again that we are learning what the kingdom of God is like or is. Jesus does things, tells us stories, does some more things, asks some questions, and we recognize these as opportunities for lessons, moments to consider. We do so because we are finite. We take in things one at a time. But what we are experiencing as we read the gospel of Luke is a little different than what happens in a classroom or what might happen if we were to hear a sermon in church centered upon a few lines of the gospel. In the very repetition with

The Gospel

a difference, in the re-formation and re-direction this repetition brings, in our considering and then reconsidering what we have read in light of what we read next, we find the gospel intruding where we may not want it. Anxious, we may even begin to find that we do not know how to get rid of it.

Luke structures his gospel to tell us what the kingdom of God is by enacting for us what the kingdom of God is doing. The kingdom of God bleeds into everything, unsettles the structures it finds, but as it breaks apart what seems to be there, it opens up room, space we could not have imagined. The kingdom of God is a consistent story, the same new life bursting through, making apparent as false structures what we hold onto just long enough for us to see and (hopefully) let go.

— III —

An Early Christmas

I love Dr. Seuss. Maybe first for his rhymes, but the illustrations come back to me, won't leave me alone. Do you remember the Grinch looking down from the mountains on a snow-lit Whoville? When, as a child reading with my little brothers, we came to this picture, I wanted to cry. Not because of the Whos' impending loss of all their presents. Maybe a little because of the sheer loneliness of it. But mainly because, though I didn't quite remember how, I had seen what the Grinch saw; I had been in those mountains. Light on snow, especially seen from a distance, comes alive as the moon bounces it across shadows of roads and buildings. Moving light, the pure joy of it (does the Grinch see this joy and not understand?), coupled with height, with distance, makes you want both to stay where you are so that you can watch forever and to go immediately into the very middle of it to feel what it is like.

Much later, reading the same story to my children, my mind sorted out some of its memories, and I realized I really had been in those mountains. Before my father adopted me, way in the early part of my life which we didn't talk about, I think because my father worried about my loving him, worried about being left out. On Christmas Eve, we would pile, with blankets and hot chocolate, into my grandparents' car and drive up above Great Falls into the foothills of the Rockies and sit in the car, looking down into town. My grandmother and grandfather let me come into the front seat,

The Gospel

and we drank cup after cup from a thermos. My grandmother in her sweet, crackly voice, would sing a Christmas carol or two.

I know now that the time we spent up there was kind of a miracle. My grandparents were deep into the process of losing their marriage. Neither of them could bear up under the weight of my grandfather's repeated infidelities. My aunt might have been there, but I don't think my mother was in the car, and I know my then father, my biological father, Pat, who must have been only twenty-one or twenty-two, did not join us. He drank and exploded. All my grandmother's Lutheran politeness could not contain him.

Years later, when I was an adult, I drove across the same mountains with Pat. We barely knew one another. He couldn't stop talking. We visited the park where Lewis and Clark saw the Great Falls, now dammed, mostly underwater. Then we went to the fish hatchery. Looking into water, I knelt down and watched, then remembered a fish swimming by when I was maybe three or four visiting the same place. Fishes were so much smaller now. Pat kept talking. When I was two, because of a false start at an Easter egg hunt, I had found an egg with one hundred dollars in it. Pat had argued with some other parents so that I could keep the money. We got in the car, headed toward Glacier, and drove and drove. And I listened. When Pat described the stir *Rebel Without a Cause* made among his friends when it came to Great Falls, I understood that he was James Dean. I couldn't say anything; he didn't pause enough to let me speak for the several hours we were in the car together, but I probably wouldn't have told him that I have never been able to get through *Rebel Without a Cause*; I think it is one of the silliest movies ever made. He wouldn't let me meet his friends at the bar. He almost didn't take a breath between words.

I wish I could remember my mother in the Christmas car, looking down at Great Falls. She is somehow just outside what I know happened. Maybe she was back at the house with my uncle putting Christmas presents under the tree. That's how I would like to picture it.

What was there, up in the mountains, under those blankets, next to my grandparents, was none of what I have just told you.

An Early Christmas

White, gold, a little red, a little green, and more white swirled around, put everything into play. Light from way down in that town in a second was on our dashboard, across the blanket, next to me. I wanted us all to follow the light into the town. Christmas was coming and was here. And even if I somehow didn't feel ready, I couldn't wait.

— IV —

Coming Into Being

IN THE NICK OF time. In the fullness of time. At the last moment, a hand reaches out to save you. At the right moment, morning breaks through. You look out your window. The night's shapelessness, its tossing and turning, has become the bright gold of autumn that was not there yesterday.

Luke opens his gospel promising to help Theophilus sort through stories, facts, deeds (or as we translate them from the Greek, "acts"), so that Theophilus (and we who read over his shoulder) might recognize a world coming into being around us. Right away, Luke gives all of us who are reading along with Theophilus action of a peculiar genus, action, he literally says, of the kind "having been fulfilled in us." "Us" points to Luke's community, to the deeds they have experienced and talked about (perhaps as they traveled around the world Luke describes in Acts), but it is also a loaded word. It can't help catching the rest of "us" up. How far exactly do the "actions having been fulfilled in us" reach? How does this "fulfilling" happen?

— V —

Becoming

*A Sermon Given at
First Presbyterian Church, Smithville*

December 23, 2018

The people walking in darkness have seen a great light; on those living in the land of deep darkness a light has dawned. You have enlarged the nation and increased their joy; they rejoice before you as people rejoice at the harvest, as warriors rejoice when dividing the plunder. For as in the day of Midian's defeat, you have shattered the yoke that burdens them, the bar across their shoulders, the rod of their oppressor. Every warrior's boot used in battle and every garment rolled in blood will be destined for burning, will be fuel for the fire. For to us a child is born, to us a son is given, and the government will be on his shoulders. And he will be called Wonderful Counselor, Mighty God, Everlasting Father, Prince of Peace. Of the greatness of his government and peace there will be no end. He will reign on David's throne and over his kingdom, establishing and upholding it with justice

The Gospel

and righteousness from that time on and forever. The zeal of the Lord Almighty will accomplish this.

ISAIAH 9:2-7 (NIV)

For the grace of the saving God has shined upon all people.

TITUS 2:11

And it became in those days, a decree went out from Caesar Augustus all the world should be registered. This first census came into being while Quirinius was governing Syria. And they all were going to register, each one to his own city. And also Joseph from Galilee, out of the city Nazareth, went up into Judea into the city of David which is called Bethlehem, on account of his being out of the house and family of David, to register with Mary, the one engaged to him, who was pregnant. And it came into being while they were there the days had been filled for her to give birth. And she gave birth to her first-born son, and she wrapped him in swaddling cloths and laid him in a manger. There was not a place for them in the inn. And shepherds were in the same country, living outdoors in the fields and guarding their flocks in the night. And an angel of the Lord stood near them, and the glory of the Lord shone around them, and they were afraid with a great fear. And the angel said to them, "Do not fear, for behold, I am bringing good news, great joy to you which will be for all the people. That a savior has been born for you today who is Christ the Lord, in the city of David. And this to you, the sign: you will find a newborn wrapped in cloths, lying in a manger. And suddenly there came into being with the angels a multitude of a

Becoming

heavenly army praising God and saying, "Glory to God in the highest and upon earth peace to men of good will." And it came into being as the angels left from them into the heaven, the shepherds were talking amongst each other. "Let us, indeed, go through immediately as far as Bethlehem, and let us see this becoming word the Lord has made known to us." And they went quickly, and they found Mary and Joseph and the newborn lying in the manger. And having seen, they made known about the words which were spoken to them about the child. And all the ones hearing wondered at the things which were spoken by the shepherds to them. But Mary kept safe all these words, throwing them together in her heart. And the shepherds returned, glorifying and praising God about all which they had heard and seen, just as it was spoken to them.

LUKE 2:1–20

Becoming

I KNOW THIS SOUNDS nutty, but most of the time, I love driving to work. Yes, our traffic is pretty hard to believe, especially for those of us who remember what it was like twenty, even just ten years ago. And yes, drivers, maybe because they are not from around here, are, at least to me, noticeably worse than they used to be. But to take part in all that flowing, moving-toward-something scramble, to see and imagine next to me nurses off to do their shifts, teachers thinking about what their classes will be like, plumbers (don't get me started on tales of our plumbing emergencies), people going to work in shops, in all the tech industries, bakers and veterinarians (my heroes), parents taking care of children; maybe a few lawyers and bankers who ought to think twice about what they are up to; okay, some good lawyers and bankers as well—I'm sure without much effort, when you are in your car and look around you, you can make your own lists—but once I get on the road, I can't help wonder at the energy we are all caught up in, cars and trucks moving along so many arteries and veins taking us to the places we do what need to do, the peculiar glory percolating up out of our everyday work.

Taxes need to be paid, so Joseph and Mary get on the road. Sheep need to be protected, so shepherds put what they will use for the night, maybe for a few days, in their bags and walk together out to the fields. Surely, Mary and Joseph's journey from Nazareth to Bethlehem, at least ninety miles, up and down cold, high, hilly country, with meeting wild animals and wild people real possibilities, was difficult for a young couple, nine months pregnant. And the shepherds—have you ever tried to help a wounded animal? What a ridiculously hard job! With, for the shepherds, such little benefit. In Palestine just before Jesus was born, shepherds, itinerant, dirty, most of them barely making enough to live, were among the lowest of the low, grouped with people like dung collectors. And yet, our shepherds were out doing what they needed to do. Joseph and Mary, no doubt a little worried or at least concerned about what would happen next to them, made the required trip to Bethlehem. They were all walking along.

It's wonderful Luke chooses to bring us Christmas by placing so many different stories next to one another. In today's twenty verses of gospel, we hear about the shepherds, Mary and Joseph, Caesar Augustus, the entire Roman world, Quirinius, the governor of Syria, a single angel, a great company of heavenly hosts, and whoever else might be at that inn and its stable. We know more people are coming in the next few verses. What a picture of the busy-ness of life, of the business of life! All that steady, swirling activity, working toward whatever is obviously next, but also, without understanding exactly how, being caught up in so much more.

In order to give us his sequences, Luke starts with, then repeats several times, words based on the Greek *genomai* throughout our gospel reading. Remember the voice of Linus in the old Charlie Brown Christmas special? "And it came to pass." That, in Greek, is *genomai*. "It came to pass"; "it happened that." Sadly, because

Becoming

these translations seem a little awkward, *genomai* is often left out of the bibles we read. Maybe also because the English words we have chosen to use can seem a little random: "I happened to get in my car and drive to work. It came to pass that you were driving too." Yet, while *genomai* is a funny idea to try to translate, it is so important that we understand at root, it means the opposite of something random. *Genomai* means "to come into being." Maybe you can hear our word, "generate" in *genomai*? The easiest way to understand *genomai* is to think about all that is involved when we say "become" or "becoming." Something begins here and is becoming and becomes what it is meant to be.

So that Luke's gospel reads: "It started becoming in those days, when Caesar Augustus made his decree," when all the Roman world was bustling about. And later: "It started becoming (or came into being) while they (Mary and Joseph) were there." And again: "it came it being while they were there that the days had been filled up for her to give birth." And another: "suddenly, there came into being with the angel, a great heavenly host, praising God." And right after: "it started becoming, as the angels left from them into heaven, the shepherds were talking amongst each other." *Genomai* all over the place. In that stable, in the field at night, during tax season, throughout the whole of the Roman empire. So that I hope, as we hear the repetition, we begin to ask ourselves: what is happening? What is coming to pass?

Isaiah tells us, "The people walking in darkness have seen a great light; on those living in the land of deep darkness a light has dawned." We may understand Isaiah to be talking about people in Israel in his own time or in Jesus's time, maybe also people living in lands of deep darkness throughout time up until and including now. This sort of seeping through time is the gift of prophecy. But let us also hear Isaiah in the very particular circumstance of our shepherds sitting out under that dark night sky. We might do so because Isaiah pictures for us simple, rural happiness, people rejoicing at the harvest, and hope for the oppressed, "the yoke that burdens them, the bar across their shoulders, the rod of their oppressor" all "shattered." Our shepherds, in the darkest night, the very bottom of a subjugated people, bear a yoke that needs shattering. We can see them, huddled together that night, maybe a little done in, shrugging their shoulders and saying, "Better get to work." Or, more quietly, "That's just how things are."

"On those living in the land of deep darkness a light has dawned." One of the miracles of Christmas is that we begin to wonder about what seems just to be. As his stories of Joseph and Mary and the shepherds come into being before our very eyes, Luke invites us to ask with him, "Is this just how things are?" We start to become a little more aware. We start to look around us.

How are we able to see the kingdom of God becoming in the places we find ourselves? Notice, the first angel in our story doesn't appear from heaven on high. Instead, "an angel of the Lord stood among them." Stood among poor, hardly thought at all about shepherds doing their work in the lonely country outside of Bethlehem. Hold onto how and where that angel came. And the next time you are looking for an angel, think about this story. Over and over again in our bible, the kingdom of God comes into being in the most unlikely places, among people who need and hope and wait for that kingdom, all the time doing the work that is front of them to do. Without knowing it, they are making themselves ready. Maybe without thinking much about it, they are open to the possibility that God's love will come flooding in.

And when the kingdom starts coming in, these people see, as we join them, we see what they and we never thought possible. "I am bringing good news, great joy to you which will be for all people." "For to us a child is born, to us a son is given. . . . And he will be called Wonderful Counselor, Mighty God, Everlasting Father, Prince of Peace." Oh, how we need a wonderful counselor, mighty God, everlasting father and prince of peace! We thought we were sitting around the campfire, about to go out again and check that all those fool sheep were where they were supposed to be, but in an instant, we find ourselves near the epicenter of the becoming kingdom of God. I'm not sure exactly how we arrived where we are; we were in such darkness, but the light that has come upon us changes how we see what we do and how we see each other. It turns out the God we have all been hoping for is real and loves us and bothers with even us poor shepherds.

So that we, along with those shepherds, might jump up and run into Bethlehem. "And it started to become as the angels went from them into heaven, the shepherds were saying to each other, 'let us now [go] as far as Bethlehem and let us see this word which has come into being (yet another *genomai*) which the Lord has made known to us.'" "The word which has come into being," or another way of saying it, a baby lying in a manger. As Mary treasures what she hears in her heart, we look into that hay and see the love of God, the very love we had always hoped for, becoming so real, right in front of us.

In an instant, as Paul says, "the grace of the saving God shines upon all." Oh, my goodness; don't you want to pick up that baby? We, who know something about what comes to pass next, might first hesitate because we feel more than a little shy. Yet standing together around the manger, taking in what all this means, we feel ourselves becoming drawn into a becoming story. Our God invites us in. Let us pick up the Christ child and look deep into that beautiful face. When we do, we will begin to see what each and all of us might become.

Amen.

— VI —

Not Whatever

In the jumble of dog walking, enjoying the park with Henry who was five and pushing Alex in the stroller, we all came to the dogs-off-the-leash stretch of the trail. Henry clapped his hands as Jack and Chloe ran first away from us down into the creek, then back, then round and round. Imitating his brother, Alex clapped his hands and reached for me to take him out. I stood him on the ground. Unstable, he laughed and tried to run in circles himself. Henry jumped to help him. In a minute, I held each one of their hands. We walked along together. Henry and I repeated stories to Alex about the fossils some students found down in the creek, about kites stuck in trees, about Jack's stealing Halloween candy and Chloe's cleaning Alex's feet.

Eight years before, I had been cautiously excited when I discovered that David and I would have a child. I was off Tegretol and had not had a seizure for a long time. I found myself waiting and telling myself "whatever." Whatever. As I think about it, I don't know how things can be whatever. Something definite always happens. When I was having seizures, I would know something was coming. I would feel wind rushing up my back, then I would be terribly afraid as if something horrible were happening in the next second, as if I were about to die. Sometimes everything I saw elongated. I still hate going into warehouses with high ceilings and tall shelves because once I had a seizure inside such a place, and the shelving that towered over me suddenly went up and up into infinity and out and out so that I was pretty sure I was trapped. And all of this because of a mosquito in Mexico. Because I wanted to see coral reefs and Chichen Itza and we stayed at a cheap hotel near the beach with lots of mosquitoes and I got dengue fever. Whatever. And I miscarried that child.

So when Henry was born two years later, it seemed like a miracle to me. I had decided that taking Tegretol for as long as I did would prevent me from having a normal pregnancy. Whatever. Then Henry opened up my whole life. And David's too. We were so thankful to God. And we were immediately and totally in love, maybe even with each other again. The epilepsy, coupled with all the pain and failure in its wake, had taken its toll on David and me. Everything Henry did was wonderful. In less than a year, he discovered poetry in his stroller as he heard the rhyme he had made up, "Oh me, oh my, oh me, oh my, trees go by." He sang, danced, wore a top hat to kindergarten. He read to me as I read to him. He seemed to understand so many things. Henry was not two years old when I brought him with me to the polls to vote. I was explaining to him how some people would be choosing Gore and some people Bush. Puzzled, he looked up at me and asked in his tiny voice, "What about Nader?"

When I hear other people's stories about how happy they are, I find myself waiting for the shoe to drop. Because the arc of everything seems to be tragic. So you need to hurry through, get to the real part, and get it over. In our dog-walking park, there really is a tree full of wrecked kites that borders on the playground. As we stood under this tree and Henry and Alex counted kites, both boys automatically took my hands again. Feeling the warmth of Alex's little fingers caught up into mine, I had the sense that something was about to happen. And then I remembered. A few years before, Henry had started talking about wanting a brother. Deep in the unbelievable joy whirling around Henry, David and I were pretty sure we shouldn't tempt things. Though I thought about it late at night a lot. And that probably is why I woke up one morning feeling like that one of my hands was empty. And that it somehow wanted to be filled. And that it should be filled.

The Gospel

And we had Alex. I think I should say we were given Alex. Sometimes heaven drips down into our lives, and sometimes we are flooded. But the water is always there, a context that we maybe don't yet recognize, one that will refigure all that has come before, one that will bring dead things to life. Alex seems to sense this more than a child his age should. Picking him up from school one day, I found him unusually quiet, then he said that he wished our leaves would change colors. When I asked him why, Alex told me about Andrew, a new boy in school from the northeast. Alex was worried that our September sun and heat would make Andrew lonely because of the fall he remembered. As we talked more and more about Andrew, Alex imagined all sorts of ways around the misery he saw coming. I found myself smiling and trusting Alex, trusting the love that rushed up out of him. Holding Alex's hand, holding Henry's hand, the grace of God has come alive for me. Of course, I do not know what will happen next, but such palpable love is enough. Enough to take me into whatever and even, I hope, to take me out again.

— VII —

Piling Up Things

DEEP INTO LUKE'S GOSPEL, we watch not so much a series of independent, digestible moments, actions, teachings, stories, but instead we find that those events, teachings, and stories bleed into one another. If words like "become" and "fulfill" repeat, accumulating and throwing off meaning as they encounter one context after another, stories, teachings, even events themselves curiously (or perhaps not so curiously) also repeat in series throughout the gospel. Each repetition provides an opportunity to re-consider what has come before as well as to use a kind of cumulative reading strategy to best respond to the story at hand.

With Luke's help, we overhear someone ask Jesus to "tell [his] brother to divide the family inheritance with [him]" (12:13). As he often does, Jesus first responds by asking a question that challenges the person in front of him: "Friend, who set me to be a judge or arbitrator over you?" (12:14). Probably, the man who believes himself wronged, who believes in the structure of wealth that Jesus ought to set right, does not hear Jesus's question. If he were to consider what Jesus asks, he might find in his own response an opening to faith, something like, "God is the one who set you to be a judge. You are set by God. Oh . . ." But the man remains silent. Jesus's question hangs in the air while Jesus tells the parable about the rich man getting richer, planning his larger and larger storehouses and barns so that he might store all of his stuff, only to die "this very night." We are humbled. We learn our lesson. And we may feel closure. The answer to the petitioner is that he should be "rich toward God" instead of storing up treasures for himself (12:21).

But having told the parable of the rich man and his barns, Jesus is not finished. When he next talks with his disciples, storehouses and barns repeat (12:24). This time, they not only are foolish, but they also become almost immaterial. Ravens have food without storehouses and barns. Value is not piled up in barns. Instead, value inhabits a much different space. "God takes care of ravens; of how much more value are you than the birds!" (12:24). Wealth moves outside of barns and storehouses and is found in you yourself. The kingdom of God busts through, levels, then fills up from the inside.

As we hear the quick stories Jesus tells, we watch, perhaps with increasing anxiety, wealth make its move. Not getting what we believe is due to us, losing those barns, being like ravens; how do we go forward in such a world? Jesus repeats "do not worry." But these repetitions invite (command?) us to act in a way that most likely does not make sense to us. We find ourselves at a crossroads. It feels like it is time to go back into and close up the barn. Pulling out from under us one security after another, Jesus forces us to consider what good going back will do. Those structures, those barns and storehouses, as well as our persistent working to get the structure of wealth right, to get all the inheritance we can and should get, more often than not, take much more than they give. We are afraid because, no matter what we do, we are somehow vulnerable. We try, but we cannot altogether protect ourselves. Our piles do not hold up. Our structures turn out to be not much help.

When Jesus repeats "do not be anxious; do not fear," we may think we are being comforted, perhaps because we want to think this, but we are also being forced to re-examine our planning those barns. Jesus speaks not to calm us down, but to direct us to a different ground: "Can any of you by worrying add a single hour to your span of life?" (12:25). For a second, we may think we have been relieved: we can stop worrying because, of course, the answer to Jesus's question is, "No, not a single hour." But Jesus's "span of life" casts a shadow over all those buildings we have been building, a shadow we cannot avoid. We thought we could build something that would make us last. That belief had us start building our own kingdoms. But we are not going to last. We are like ravens. We are like flowers. There is that span of life Jesus tells us about, measured in hours.

We become more and more uneasy. Again, what should we do? "Make purses for yourselves that do not wear out, an unfailing treasure in heaven, where no thief comes near and no moth destroys" (12:32). Weak-kneed, we may feel we have had enough and hope to rest here, considering unfailing treasure (vs. the treasure of inheritance; vs. the treasure in the barns; vs. the treasure of Solomon). But again, Jesus is not finished. We meet, in a following parable, another rich owner of the house who does not know how to plan. And another thief. Two more repetitions with a difference. Here, the owner of the house has not planned for the thief (12:39). And the Son of Man is the thief. Should we be glad that the owner cannot protect himself? The logic of the passage (in so far as we can call it logic) suggests that we should. Our barns, our storehouses, our treasures, our houses, our asserting and fighting for our place in the structure of wealth, all are and need to be disrupted, broken into, undone. Our structures will not hold. Jesus, the thief, takes everything away from us. Presumably, for our own good.

We may now hear with a difference, hear as a question to answer and as an answer to wonder at: "Friend, who set me to be a judge or an arbitrator over you?" Each of these words requires our attention: "friend" (Jesus, in his mercy, calls us this), "who" (I thought it was me, but who was it?), "set/stood me against" (Who is Jesus and why is he here and why do I feel like he is set against me? Is he a thief?), "me" (That Jesus standing in front of me requires his own space), "a judge," (The one who will take away my barns; Is he my friend?), "an arbitrator," (Should I argue when I have nothing?), "over you" (Is this teacher over me? Will I listen to him?). Reading through the stories that follow from this question, we begin to realize that our resolute stance, our own building up and hunkering down into those barns, all our money, will not hold us up under pressure. We may find ourselves watching the new wine burst through, licking our wounds, imagining for ourselves how good the old wine was.[1] But we may also glimpse, for a moment, the beginnings of the outline of something new.

---

[1]. Comparing Luke to Mark and Matthew shows the intensity of Luke's conception. Neither Mark nor Matthew contains the parable of the rich fool. Matthew chapter 6 collects as Jesus's sayings both Jesus's advice about storing up treasures on earth and his advice about not worrying with an interlude in between them. Only Luke moves from the parable of the rich fool through barns and storehouses to worry and the thief in the night.

— VIII —

Collapse

SOMETIME IN 2008 (OR was it 2009?), within a month, three large projects that were to fund our clinic for the next year were cancelled or postponed. Two, three, four, five . . . times a day, I asked David if he or if anyone else at the clinic had heard about a fourth project that was supposed to be starting in a few weeks. The few weeks became a month. Then two. Then three. Then that project also was postponed indefinitely.

 At the time, our clinic provided hope and a safe place for more than a thousand patients with schizophrenia and other mental illnesses. We employed thirty-four people. Our monthly expenses ran between $225,000–250,000. We had been up and running for fifteen years. Our staff, dedicated to our patients and to our work, had become not only people with whom I worked but my extended family. Trying to keep the clinic afloat, we began to go into our line of credit. Our clients said work might be around the corner, but no work came. And we ran through most of our accounts receivable and took care of our patients and tried to not to let anyone go. We made up work for the staff. And suddenly we were $500,000 in debt, and the bank would not give us any more money.

 During this time, I suffered from profound insomnia. Every night, I spent time with Henry and Alex, took a bath, watched television, tried to read, then the moment I lay in bed, I was wide awake. At times, I didn't sleep at all for two or even three days.

The Gospel

Breathless, I replayed in my mind how, if only we were to receive a certain call or if my calculations were not correct or if we moved around debt, we might be able to salvage the clinic. Sometimes my mind took me (I very much felt as if I were a hostage) to places in which I didn't recognize myself. I thought about how embarrassing it would be to move, how hard it would be to see acquaintances at the grocery store or the pool or the movies, how much we needed what we had in order to protect our children. Before long, I would get out of bed, walk around our house, and imagine myself into just how devastating it would be to take Henry and Alex out of their schools. The more I thought about those schools, the more it seemed like, no matter what, we had to keep Henry and Alex in them. At the same time, I would start planning curricula for both of them so that I would be ready to teach them at home if I needed to while we were moving and figuring things out. Could I really handle Calculus? I kept thinking about going to Montana. And about teaching. I wanted so much to go back to teaching, but I could never make enough money to dig us out of our debt. David and I could never make enough money. Somehow David slept. I knew waking him up wouldn't help, but sometimes I tried to wake him up anyway.

Of course, I prayed in bursts. If I went outside and sat on our balcony and felt the wind on my face, I might fall asleep for a few hours. But waking up in the dark of the night, I started my calculations again. While I added, subtracted, moved numbers around, some muffled part of me would try to say "God, help me, help me, help me." Without acknowledging it, I would hear my own voice mouthing these words, but then I would return to all those numbers.

And here's the funny part: David and I had built up quite a pile, though we never much thought of what we had as a pile. We had a small farm where we were slowly building a barn to move our horses; we had built a great house in the middle of Austin; we had put money away into retirement accounts. If the financial chaos going on in the world had beaten back considerably the value of all this stuff, it still had value. At a certain point, when it looked like we could negotiate our debt no further, all of our

Collapse

stuff became stuff to me. The farm, the house, the saved money connected to our thoughts about what we would do when we were not working, had never been stuff to me before. You would think having this stuff would be comforting. But feeling the things that I loved become the quickly diminishing pile underneath us was excruciating. What were we going to do with the horses? Not to mention, the schools. How were we going to lose everything and take care of everyone we loved?

Where was God in all this? A reasonable enough question, but I am ashamed to say I only asked it when I was counting. Please God, when will that stupid call come in? We began negotiating with a group of investors who wanted to buy the clinic. Somehow, I connected God to the ups and downs of our negotiations. And I fretted David, fretted him relentlessly, while I wrote narratives for the investors, compiled the lists upon lists they asked for, and worked through our financials. David had found a manic banker who was willing to consolidate our debt and loan us more money. I started talking to a realtor about selling our house. The cost of doing business with the manic banker was my being required to listen to him weekly, but the realtor was more useful. She connected me with her husband, a mortgage broker, and he refinanced our house. Weeks went by. David didn't like the investors; they said things like, "You have twenty beds; look how much more money you could bring in if you did something a little different; if they were full." What our clinic represented to us: the people, the science, being on the edge of a breakthrough for those suffering with schizophrenia, all of this somehow was beside the point to the group of men who visited us and then to the second group of men who followed them. After a month or so, David told me that he wanted to keep the clinic like it was or just to go bankrupt. But he didn't think we would go bankrupt.

Everybody else did.

The investors left. I still wasn't sleeping. You couldn't tell me anything I didn't know about our situation. Our dear friend, Don, stayed with us for awhile. After dinner, we would sit and talk, and Don would say, "It's going to be okay," and then he would enter into

The Gospel

my numbers, and we would concoct some method of extracting a little more out of nothing. All of us adults would imagine moving out to the farm and laugh a little. Don and I talked about going to seminary. And Don sat with me, even begrudgingly watched TV with me, in the midst of his own crises, financial and otherwise.

When you look around (which I didn't), there are no shortage of crises. During this time, my friend, Alida, was slowly dying of ovarian cancer, though whenever she went to a doctor and was told she only had months or even weeks, she lived another year, I think just to prove the doctor wrong. Because her cancer had returned with a vengeance, I ended up with Willie, a giant, terrified, highly bred five-year-old Trakehner whom Alida had never managed to start under saddle. The day I broke my arm when he whirled around and reared because a door slammed, Alida came running. Practically a skeleton, she leaned over me and said, "I'll ride him. I'll do it." A button in her shirt broke so I could see her clavicle bones pointing to the port stuck into her chest in order give her chemo. I just lay there on the ground.

That day led me to Susie, who took me and Willie in while I left my other horses with Alida so I could stay in her life too. Susie plopped a Western saddle on Willie's back, and the three of us worked together week after week. All through the horrible summer then fall when we were waiting to hear whether or not our clinic projects would start, Susie and I rode together. Willie became Willie at Susie's. When he was born, in keeping with her hopes for him, Alida had named him "Willwadar," with the "w" pronounced as a "v" in good Tex-Deutch-Dressage fashion. He was supposed to be as brave as she was, but no one could be. Jumping six feet in the air anytime he was surprised by his shadow, Willie was nowhere near brave. Worse, he seemed to only remember you where there when he was able to be calm, so he was dangerous. But Susie and I rode and rode and tried to let him know we were in it together.

A couple of months after Willie and I arrived, we had worked our way to loping around Susie's arena. I was frightened and sweating. Susie yelled to me, "Drop the reins." I told her no. She kept after me: "You're holding him; your reins are too tight. Just drop

Collapse

them. You'll be fine." I knew I could not handle the power and terror of this horse when he came unglued, but, seeing Susie's smiling face, somehow, I dropped the reins. We were going faster than I had ever gone, round the outside of the arena. I let the reins fall on Willie's neck. I didn't know what to do with my hands, so, for a minute, I put them on my head. We kept running. Willie stretched out, and I expected him to go even faster, to buck, to swerve. I expected to be flying. But he fell into the most even, graceful, beautiful lope I have ever ridden. Really.

You tell me where God was then. We had to spread out the building of our barn so that it took almost three years. I got to spend all that time with Susie. And Don. And Alida. And David. And Henry. And Alex. And so many others. At the clinic, Mark and I worried together and moved work around enough for us to limp through. A few people left. Kathleen came in one day and said she wanted a pay cut. It was a dry, dusty time. Two weeks before Alida died, she had a huge birthday party for her husband Sam. She said good-bye to everyone, and Sam picked her up out of her wheel chair, and they danced. When you get to the end of something, you still have a choice. At that moment, you may look back (I have looked back) and see all your fear and mistakes and foolishness. But I also see something else. The help I needed wasn't where I thought it should be. But it was there nevertheless. No one who has seen Susie's smile or heard her laugh could doubt it.

— IX —

Locating Hope

*A Sermon Given to
Genesis Presbyterian Church, Austin*

August 7, 2017

After this, the word of the Lord came to Abram in a vision: "Do not be afraid, Abram. I am your shield, your very great reward." But Abram said, "Sovereign Lord, what can you give me since I remain childless and the one who will inherit my estate is Eliezer of Damascus?" And Abram said, "You have given me no children; so a servant in my household will be my heir." Then the word of the Lord came to him: "This man will not be your heir, but a son who is your own flesh and blood will be your heir." He took him outside and said, "Look up at the sky and count the stars—if indeed you can count them." Then he said to him, "So shall your offspring be." Abram believed the Lord, and he credited it to him as righteousness.

GENESIS 15:1-6 (NIV)

Locating Hope

Now faith is the substance of things hoped for, the evidence of things not seen. For by it the elders obtained a good report. Through faith we understand that the worlds were framed by the word of God, so that things which are seen were not made of things which do appear.

By faith Abraham, when he was called to go out into a place which he should after receive for an inheritance, obeyed; and he went out, not knowing whither he went. By faith he sojourned in the land of promise, as in a strange country, dwelling in tabernacles with Isaac and Jacob, the heirs with him of the same promise: For he looked for a city which hath foundations, whose builder and maker is God. Through faith also Sara herself received strength to conceive seed, and was delivered of a child when she was past age, because she judged him faithful who had promised. Therefore sprang there even of one, and him as good as dead, so many as the stars of the sky in multitude, and as the sand which is by the sea shore innumerable. These all died in faith, not having received the promises, but having seen them afar off, and were persuaded of them, and embraced them, and confessed that they were strangers and pilgrims on the earth. For they that say such things declare plainly that they seek a country. And truly, if they had been mindful of that country from whence they came out, they might have had opportunity to have returned. But now they desire a better country, that is, an heavenly: wherefore God is not ashamed to be called their God: for he hath prepared for them a city.

HEBREWS 11:1–3, 8–16 (KJV)

The Gospel

"Do not be afraid, little flock, for your Father has been pleased to give you the kingdom. Sell your possessions and give to the poor. Provide purses for yourselves that will not wear out, a treasure in heaven that will never fail, where no thief comes near and no moth destroys.

For where your treasure is, there your heart will be also. *"Be dressed ready for service and keep your lamps burning, like servants waiting for their master to return from a wedding banquet, so that when he comes and knocks they can immediately open the door for him. It will be good for those servants whose master finds them watching when he comes. Truly I tell you, he will dress himself to serve, will have them recline at the table and will come and wait on them. It will be good for those servants whose master finds them ready, even if he comes in the middle of the night or toward daybreak. But understand this: If the owner of the house had known at what hour the thief was coming, he would not have let his house be broken into. You also must be ready, because the Son of Man will come at an hour when you do not expect him."*

LUKE 12:32–40 (NIV)

Locating Hope

WHAT DO YOU HOPE for? If we went around the room, we might hear as answers to this question: I hope for health. I hope to see a loved one. I hope for a better job. We hope for relief after horrible storms, for peace and kindness in our nation and in the world. Maybe some of us already are starting to hope for the Longhorns next year. I could easily spend the rest of the morning listing my own big hopes and small hopes, and we could talk about how much or how little our hopes depend upon our own actions. But I want, for a second, to press harder on this question. What do you hope for? Why bother hoping?

I suppose we ought to start by just facing something uncomfortable. Our lists of all those things we hope for—you and I are most likely not going to end up with at least some of what is on them. We probably won't get what we want when we want or how we want. But most of us go on hoping anyway. Why? Where does this come from?

In his conversation with God, Abram hears God speak what he has hoped for, even more than he has hoped for: "Look up at the sky and count the stars—if indeed you can count them. So shall your offspring be." We can imagine how stunning this is. Before this moment, Abram and Sarah, childless and far too old to expect children, see as their future an end that feels like oblivion. No one coming after them. No connection to what will be. When Abram tells God, "You have given me no children," Abram speaks his most severe disappointment. If he were just talking to himself, listening to himself, alone, Abram would have been at an end. But Abram is not talking to himself. "Look up at the sky and count the stars—if indeed you can count them." In an instant, God, having heard Abram, catches him up in the mystery and magic of the universe. In that instant, Abram finds a God who is paying attention.

If Abram's story teaches us anything, it teaches us that the very least (and perhaps the very best) thing we can do is take our complaints, our fears, our hopes and disappointments directly to God. We don't have to look very hard in Scripture to find the God Abram knows. Remember Mary bothering Jesus about the wine for the wedding in Cana. Remember what happened? Jesus's first miracle in the gospel of John is making water into wine for that wedding party. We can marvel at all the healings, the walking on water, feeding the multitudes that come next. But Jesus starts with a miracle responding to everyday needs, everyday hopes. While, of course, God is not our sugar daddy, our pocket genie who makes things work out the way we want them, our faith encourages us to use our hope muscle, to use it about big things and small things. When we do so, we might smile and remember Abram's stars and the wine at that party. Hope that connects us to God may lead us to all sorts of places.

But maybe not to the places we were expecting. Hebrews reminds us that Abram chooses to be a stranger in a strange land. The land where we are heading may look strange to us, not because of what it is in itself, but because of the way we are looking at it. Jesus's comfort may not feel like comfort: "Do not fear, little flock, because the father has thought it good to give you the kingdom. Sell your existing things and give alms. Make for yourselves purses that do not wear out, an unfailing treasure house in heaven where neither thief comes near nor a moth ruins." As we contemplate what might be involved for each of us in making purses that do not wear out, we may forget where Jesus started, "the father has thought it good to give you the kingdom." The benefit of directing our hope toward those things that we know will help bring in God's kingdom is, well, that we will be closer to living in that kingdom. The very kingdom that, though we may not know it, is exactly the place we need to be. The very kingdom that we sometimes choose not to enter because of the ridiculous treasure, both physical and otherwise, we have dragging us down and back.

Far too often, we ground our hopes in the life we try to force for ourselves, in all the structures we keep building around us. Jesus tells us that if we had known a thief was coming, we would have been able to keep him out. At first, when we read this in the gospel, it seems odd. Jesus himself is coming like a thief in the night: should we try to keep him out, stay inside, lock all the doors, batten down the hatches? Probably not. But when our hopes are turning us in the wrong direction, we are trying to do something like this. We busy ourselves; we hope and hope we can hold what we have together, lock the doors, store up some more, but where does all of this get us? Besides being frustrated, we end up a little foolish when we try to hold out in the forts we build and direct our hopes toward maintaining them. Because Jesus is risen and is coming. We are not going to be able to keep him out.

So we may hope, we should exercise our hope muscles, but at the same time we must remember where we are. I don't mean

Locating Hope

remember that we are in a place where we don't have what we hope for. I mean remember, even in our worst circumstances, that God has thought it good to give us the kingdom. Not necessarily the stuff we want at a particular moment. But the kingdom. The love, beauty, joy, compassion, justice, and peace we all long for. If we are paying attention, what we start to see about the act of hoping is that it is able to connect us to the places God wants us to inhabit. Maybe in a sort of roundabout way, at least at first. But, without thinking more than a couple of minutes, each of us might tell our own story about a hope fulfilled beyond what we thought possible and of where that hope led; we might also remember a disappointment that turned around, that was the best thing for us. When we consider these moments, we discover that we are on a journey. Our hopes, even our disappointments, make sense to us as we understand them in the context of this journey, of getting us to a place God is preparing.

Perhaps we go out like Abram, full of hope, but not exactly knowing where we will find the place we hope for. Hebrews tells us that Abram set off by faith. That picture of a person walking along in the desert, hoping, because of faith, thinking about all those stars in the sky, can be a picture of us if we want it to be. To walk in faith is to step out on the substance of things hoped for, the evidence of things not seen. For "substance," Hebrews uses the curious word *hypostasis*, literally, standing underneath. Faith is the thing which stands underneath and holds up hope. Even more, the word *hypostasis* insists that faith refers to something really there, a necessary substructure. Maybe this is too old an image, but think about the groove in the record in which the needle must rest in order for us to hear music. Our hopes are that music. Faith is the foundation upon which I can hope with confidence and hope toward what is the best for me, for you, for the world.

Faith is not only what is underneath, but also somehow the sure proof of deeds we have not seen. How can this be? Maybe a better question is: how can you have faith in the world that you do see? We know this world to be a mess, too often an unspeakably sad, tragic place. We may talk about a sort of automatic faith or trust we have in our senses, but this trust gets us only so far. A ball will always drop when you let it go, but what will your neighbor do next? The things that we see and the things that we know do not coincide exactly with what it is we should trust.

Indeed, the world we live in all too often works toward undermining our hope and our faith. It always has. Think for a minute about the hope that must have surrounded Jesus as he walked through Israel and Samaria healing and teaching. Can you imagine it? Maybe as you remember the sick in your life, the addicted, the broken-hearted. When you consider the cross from the point of view of anybody who has real needs, you can almost hear the horrible violence of all that hope being shattered. If this were the end of the story, we would not know who Jesus was. None of us could have imagined the reality of Easter, the odd combination of substance and evidence, a man whom we need so badly, who did things and told us things that made us hope, the same man, having been brutally murdered, standing alive among us. Because of Easter, in our darkest moments, we can hope and hope in a new way. And down underneath that hope, we are able to find trust, faith strong enough to hold us up. And let us go on hoping. Even while we see clearly the world in which we live.

Because of Easter, we can hope for and work with confidence toward God's kingdom come. While we may not know where we are going next or what might happen to us, we know where we are headed. And who is there. In Jesus's story today, the master of the house is out celebrating at a wedding. He comes home late at night and sees all of his earnest, busy servants. He pulls on the clothes he needs to serve, has everyone sit, literally recline at the table, and waits upon them. That is our God. The same God who tells Abram, "Do not be afraid. I am your shield, your very great reward." Inviting us in, waiting upon us, even surprising us with joy, God would have us locate our hope, well, in God. Longing for the overwhelming love, wisdom, peace, justice, compassion and care that calls us, let us take up this precious invitation.

Amen.

— X —

Breaking Us Open

You and I are moving targets, jumping from story to story, none of which holds together for very long. And yet we hope; I hope. We believe that, through it all, at least our selves remain intact. I might plan what I intend to be the next good parts of my life. You might follow a thread and see yourself continuing back, back into your childhood.

And then I sit down again to read. What happens next I often do not expect. My reading bogs down; I begin to see things repeating that don't exactly repeat. Caught up in Luke's gospel, I start to notice how Luke insists that I pause, that I hear and hear again what I am doing, thinking, saying. Every so gently, then with sudden brawniness, Luke takes me, takes us, apart as he picks our stories up.

In Luke, repetition, bleed among stories, destabilizes, then breaks open our understanding, our landscapes. In chapter 15, we have three "losts": after Jesus's parable of the lost sheep comes the parable of the lost coin then the parable of the lost son.[1] At first, we identify with the joy which the one who does the finding

---

1. The parables of the lost coin and prodigal son are unique to the gospel of Luke. While Matthew contains the parable of the lost sheep, Matthew places this parable within the context of not "despising one of these little ones" (Matt 18:10–14). The sheep become lost children who need to be brought to Jesus: "So it is not the will of your Father in heaven that one of these little ones should be lost" (Matt 18:14).

experiences, the shepherd, the woman with the coins. Jesus directs us to connect that joy to the joy in heaven over one person who repents (and is therefore no longer lost). So we think we are done. Heaven wants us not to be lost.

Mindful of the finder's joy, we then enter into the story of the prodigal son, and we meet lostness from the point of view of the lost, from the sinner who needs to repent. With the story of the prodigal son, we repeat the lost story, get it from another point of view, perhaps so that we will discover the misery of our own lostness. In this way, repetition allows Jesus to call us out of our sin to repentance, but, most important, this repentance is within the context of how much the finder wants us not to be lost, how happy heaven will be when we are found. The father catches up his lost son in his arms; we have the joy and think we have come full circle.

But the parable of the prodigal son contains repetition with a difference. A second son enters. And we end with this angry, jealous son confronting his father. The father reaches out, encourages his older son to join in the celebration. But will the son come to the party? How far does the joy reach?

— XI —

My Dad And Me

W%%HEN I BECAME A%% Christian, it about killed my Dad. Angry, he told me that I would grow out of it. What he meant was that I would grow out of being rebellious. What he meant was that he was horribly hurt. I didn't know what else to say, so I asked him what he thought about God. He said God was something people made up because they needed to make God up, because they were afraid, because they were weak.

For a second, I took this as a blow. After all, I was afraid (I was pretty sure my father knew this); I was weak. My father's mouth was tight, his face closed. I wanted to tell him that he was right, just put the whole thing behind us. But really what he said didn't make sense. Well, maybe rationally it did. But why had we lived our lives the way we had lived them?

Before my parents' divorce, when we were a family, we went to temple, maybe not every week but at least every so often. When we moved to Texas, Dad took me to Saturday school at the temple; he hoped I would be bat mitzvahed. We fasted on Yom Kippur. We celebrated Rosh Hashanah. Earlier, as a child, I could see Mount Vesuvius from my bedroom window, and during the holy days, as I thought about my sins, I could feel the volcano about to erupt. I would plan never to sin again. But the next day . . . . The whole business was hopeless.

Hopeless and yet oddly cheerful. At Passover, the few American Jews in Naples would collect at our apartment for a Seder. Dad

The Gospel

would sing and grate potatoes all morning. Eric rolled around the tiled kitchen in his walker, and I sat chopping onions. Having eaten matzah and more matzah leading up to Passover, I thought a lot about peanut butter and jelly sandwiches. But those potato pancakes made up for everything, even for having to eat lamb, even for the bitter herbs. At night, we all sat around our living room, and my father read the Seder. He told the story of the four questioners. And the horrible son who asks, "What did God do for them?" Everyone present seemed to understand that this was an awful question, that the son should have asked, "What did God do for us?" But I squirmed in my seat. If I didn't know better, I might have asked a wrong question, said "them," not "us," because those Hebrews in Egypt were people who lived a long time ago. How did you know for sure that you are saying the right thing, that you are asking the right questions?

My grandmother, my father, my uncle, my aunt, all my Jewish relatives, were so confident about God. God was okay with us. Scary. But okay. And then my father told me that he did not believe in God. I still don't know what to think about what he said.

Why does what we say bind us? Words in the air. When my mother was living with her fourth husband, the one she married instead of remarrying my Dad, she and this man eventually moved out of the house my Dad had bought for her and went to Dallas. I had just learned how to drive, and Dad decided to give me his old car. He drove from Shreveport to the parking lot in front of the place where my mother and her husband lived. He didn't say much. We started driving; the car had a stick shift, and he was intent upon my learning how to use the clutch. Clumsy and nervous, I grated the gears more than once. We went out onto a busy road. The car stalled at a light. I couldn't figure out how to get it started. Dad began to yell. He yelled before the light, after we were driving again, and was still yelling when I stalled out a second time. Finally, I shouted back, "Take your car. I don't need it. I won't drive it." Traffic piled up behind us; we changed seats, and Dad drove me back to my mother's condo. I don't think he came in; he just left for his hotel. I couldn't figure out how to pay for a car, so I rode my bike through college and into graduate school. We somehow let that happen.

How? When Dad was being treated for cancer about ten years ago, the doctor pointed to a scar across his stomach and into his chest and mumbled something about "old school" spleen surgery. Throughout my childhood, we had heard all sorts of stories about that scar. My Dad was in different versions of a knife fight in New York, or he somehow was wounded in combat. Standing behind my dad during that horrible doctor's visit, I found out that in high school he had leukemia. He was hospitalized most of his sophomore year; they were certain that he was going to die. This was after his Dad had died suddenly of a heart attack, which had thrown his family into grief and poverty. After he wasn't bar mitzvahed. After his world had fallen apart. We left the doctor's office, and Dad laughed as he told me when he was sixteen, he woke from surgery to his mother's arguing over his body with a Catholic priest. The priest mistakenly had come in to perform the last rites, and my father says his mother was yelling, "We're Jewish; we're Jewish."

My father lived with his mother and brother, worked his way through college, took care of his mother and grudgingly let her take care of him, then ran away from home and the life his mother planned for him, the girl she had hoped he would marry, his being a pharmacist in the city. Without telling anyone, he joined the Air Force and went to Montana. And lived it up. And met my mother.

And then brought me with my mother to Yonkers. I lived with Grandma Rose for a few months while Dad was overseas. My mother was there for a bit, then she left. I'm not sure if she went back to Montana or somewhere else. During our time together, Grandma Rose fell in love with me, and I fell in love with her. We went all over New York. We met Aunt Miriam at Lee's Chinese where kosher rules did not exist, so we could eat sweet pork spare ribs ("When you are in Rome, honey, you have to do what the Romans do"). Grandma Rose took me to Caravel Ice Cream, to Macy's, to Coney Island, to see the ocean, to feed the pigeons at the foot of the statue of the man riding the horse. And sent me packages when we moved to Italy. And saved her money to visit us. And kept loving me until she died.

When Dad left for Montana, it must have broken Grandma Rose's heart. I don't think she ever stopped worrying about him. Right after the divorce, we visited her in Florida. She had leukemia, but it was my Dad who looked sick. His skin was so grey. My brothers probably were too young to remember, but she wanted to take us to Orlando; she wanted to buy me clothes. I got a t-shirt with Groucho Marx's face on it. She laughed and laughed. "Did I really know who he was?" My Dad was quiet, tired. She made all of us rice pudding. We went to delis in Florida that reminded her of New York, and then Dad took us back to Texas. I never saw her again.

After she died, I visited New York more than once with my father. My uncle and aunt orchestrated for us eating tours through the city. Cannolis, Chinese noodles, rugelach, Rockefeller Center, ice cream. As we walked and drove and walked, my uncle was our constant guide: "this is where our father worked"; "this is where your father and me went to school"; "this is where we caught the bus downtown." My Dad half-heartedly went along. Then we came to Randolph Street. The apartment building where his family had lived was horribly run-down. As we drove past, as my uncle told us stories about his mother's kugle and about my Dad sneaking in late at night and always being caught, I opened my window to see if I could remember anything. Grandma Rose's clucking and humming and nodding her head came to me along with the dumbwaiter in the kitchen that took the garbage down to the basement, the plastic covering the good furniture in the living room we avoided, my grandmother sitting at her kitchen table and making me food and apologizing for being kosher so that maybe the mashed potatoes didn't taste right to me? My father, in the seat in front of me, was also looking intently out the window. I don't think anyone else noticed, but tears were streaming down his face. I don't think he knew, but I was crying too.

My Grandmother Rose kept everything together and forced her love to go as far as it would go. As my brother and I sat with my father during his cancer treatments, I know he was thinking about what it was like when he had been at the hospital with her. We were waiting to be called for his spinal tap. Shuffling some cards someone had placed strategically in order to distract those of us waiting, Jason tried to remember the rules of Uno. We heard an adult man screaming in pain on the other side of the door. I felt sick to my stomach. My Dad looked at us both, and when he smiled, his mother smiled through his eyes. I think he knew how much I loved him, how much we loved him. Then they called his name. He marched up to the door. He may have said, "yes, sir," to the nurse. As they took him back, I wanted so badly for all of us to go home.

— XII —

Taking In Forgiveness

*A Sermon Given to
First Presbyterian Church, Smithville*

March 24, 2019

*Happy are those whose transgression is forgiven,
whose sin is covered.*

*Happy are those to whom the Lord imputes no iniquity,
and in whose spirit there is no deceit.*

*While I kept silence, my body wasted away
through my groaning all day long.*

*For day and night your hand was heavy upon me;
my strength was dried up as by the heat of summer.*

*Then I acknowledged my sin to you, and I did not hide
my iniquity; I said, "I will confess my transgressions to
the Lord," and you forgave the guilt of my sin.*

*Therefore let all who are faithful offer prayer to you; at a
time of distress, the rush of mighty waters
shall not reach them.*

Taking In Forgiveness

You are a hiding place for me; you preserve me from trouble; you surround me with glad cries of deliverance.

I will instruct you and teach you the way you should go; I will counsel you with my eye upon you.

Do not be like a horse or a mule, without understanding, whose temper must be curbed with bit and bridle, else it will not stay near you.

Many are the torments of the wicked, but steadfast love surrounds those who trust in the Lord.

Be glad in the Lord and rejoice, O righteous, and shout for joy, all you upright in heart.

PSALM 32 (NRSV)

From now on, therefore, we regard no one from a human point of view; even though we once knew Christ from a human point of view, we know him no longer in that way. So if anyone is in Christ, there is a new creation: everything old has passed away; see, everything has become new! All this is from God, who reconciled us to himself through Christ, and has given us the ministry of reconciliation; that is, in Christ God was reconciling the world to himself, not counting their trespasses against them, and entrusting the message of reconciliation to us. So we are ambassadors for Christ, since God is making his appeal through us; we entreat you on behalf of Christ, be reconciled to God. For our sake he made him to be sin who knew no sin, so that in him we might become the righteousness of God.

2 CORINTHIANS 5:16–21 (NRSV)

The Gospel

Now all the tax collectors and sinners were coming near to listen to him. And the Pharisees and the scribes were grumbling and saying, "This fellow welcomes sinners and eats with them." So he told them this parable:

"There was a man who had two sons. The younger of them said to his father, 'Father, give me the share of the property that will belong to me.' So he divided his property between them. A few days later the younger son gathered all he had and traveled to a distant country, and there he squandered his property in dissolute living. When he had spent everything, a severe famine took place throughout that country, and he began to be in need. So he went and hired himself out to one of the citizens of that country, who sent him to his fields to feed the pigs. He would gladly have filled himself with the pods that the pigs were eating; and no one gave him anything. But when he came to himself he said, 'How many of my father's hired hands have bread enough and to spare, but here I am dying of hunger! I will get up and go to my father, and I will say to him, "Father, I have sinned against heaven and before you; I am no longer worthy to be called your son; treat me like one of your hired hands."' So he set off and went to his father. But while he was still far off, his father saw him and was filled with compassion; he ran and put his arms around him and kissed him. Then the son said to him, 'Father, I have sinned against heaven and before you; I am no longer worthy to be called your son.' But the father said to his slaves, 'Quickly, bring out a robe—the best one—and put it on him; put a ring on his finger and sandals on his feet. And get the fatted calf and kill it and let us eat and celebrate; for this son of mine was dead and is alive again; he was lost and is found!' And they began to

celebrate. "Now his elder son was in the field; and when he came and approached the house, he heard music and dancing. He called one of the slaves and asked what was going on. He replied, 'Your brother has come, and your father has killed the fatted calf, because he has got him back safe and sound.' Then he became angry and refused to go in. His father came out and began to plead with him. But he answered his father, 'Listen! For all these years I have been working like a slave for you, and I have never disobeyed your command; yet you have never given me even a young goat so that I might celebrate with my friends. But when this son of yours came back, who has devoured your property with prostitutes, you killed the fatted calf for him!' Then the father said to him, 'Son, you are always with me, and all that is mine is yours. But we had to celebrate and rejoice, because this brother of yours was dead and has come to life; he was lost and has been found.'"

LUKE 15:1–3, 11–32 (NRSV)

Taking in Forgiveness

WHAT DOES FORGIVENESS FEEL like to you? As you think about your answer, I wonder if you are the forgiver or forgiven in what comes first to your mind? I suppose I can go both ways; I can remember both types of situations. Yet one is so much more immediate for me, so much more powerful. The release that happens when I do not receive the bad that I should have coming, that is something I understand deep down in my bones.

When I was seven, I spent most days in the summer outside, playing kickball, running around with a group of friends, only going home for lunch, then later once it started getting dark. There were lots of things I was not supposed to do. Among them was to walk down a busy road just outside of our neighborhood, cross the railroad tracks, and end up at the beach. So of course, one very hot day, an older kid talked my group of friends into doing exactly this. As I darted through traffic, I heard my father's voice, "You can play all day, but you can't leave the neighborhood." Hmmm. Each of us saw the train in the distance. Then we ran across the tracks. I felt sick to my stomach. The beach we came to was sludgy and not that much fun because none of us were wearing bathing suits. Someone picked up a big twisted conch shell. After I had put it up to my ear to listen to it, an older girl grabbed it out of my hand and threw it as far as she could. It turned out, someone had told her and everyone agreed, that this was the kind of shell that had a fatal bacteria in it, left behind by its old occupant. And the way the bacteria got into you was by putting the shell up to your ear.

Aaagh! I spent our walk back across the railroad tracks, down that busy street, all the way past broken up potato fields then into our neighborhood, in terror. At home, I washed my face, splashed water in my ear, and waited. I couldn't believe what I had done. I was too preoccupied to eat much dinner. So I went into my room and laid down in my bed and waited again for something to happen. The relief I felt when I figured out that I was still living made me laugh and cry and promise myself that I would never, never, never leave the neighborhood. When I finally told my father what I had done, he saw how very worried I was and decided that I had been punished enough. I felt like I was starting over. And that starting over was everything in the world to me.

Oh, what it is to be forgiven! "Happy are those whose transgression is forgiven, whose sin is covered." Happy, indeed. Those of us who know what it is to be forgiven, who have spent some time with the pigs, understand the younger son in Jesus's parable. "But when he came to himself he said, 'how many of my father's hired hands have bread enough and to spare, but here I am dying of hunger! I will get up and go to my father, and I will say to him, Father, I have sinned against heaven and before you; I am no longer worthy to be called your son; treat me like one of your hired hands.'" Do you hear the desperation in "I have sinned against heaven and before you?" To know that your choices have taken away your happiness, to know that you yourself have ruined your life, to know, even worse, that you have hurt others, that you have taken away from them joy, peace, or maybe more, that you have taken parts of their lives that are most important to them; when all of this crashes down upon you, upon me, what are we to do?

Just to be clear, the stakes in our gospel story are higher than we might have first thought. When the younger son asks the father to give him money so that he can set out on his adventure, in the Greek, he asks for *ousias*, property, belongings, but in the next sentence the word changes. Jesus tells us that the father divides his *bios*, his life (it is a pity translations use the word "property" again) between his two sons so that the younger son is able to leave. The younger son is taking *bios*, is taking life from his father. As he wastes away all that he has been given, he pulls down not just himself, but those who love him, those he ought to love, along with him.

Hear our psalmist: "For day and night your hand was heavy upon me; my strength was dried up as by the heat of summer. Then I acknowledged my sin to you, and I did not hide my iniquity." Our younger son's story is an old, old, old one. And one that is right now, probably in this room somewhere. We hurt ourselves. We hurt those we love. We hurt those we don't even know. We need forgiveness.

So that surely our hearts leap up as we hear and hear again in Paul: "All this is from God, who reconciled us to himself through Christ." "In Christ, God was reconciling the world to himself." "For our sake he made him to be sin who knew no sin, so that in him we might become the righteousness of God." We ask for forgiveness. We hope we might be allowed to live out in the barn with the hired hands, work, and eat our bit of bread. We don't actually deserve this; we just hope for it. But then, our father comes running down the street with his arms open wide. "So if anyone is in Christ, there is a new creation; everything old has passed away; see everything has become new!" Forgiveness is the miracle we could not have imagined. Love, new life, starting again as beloved children.

Who doesn't long for this? What might God do so that we are able to come on home? And yet, sometimes when we hear the word "forgiveness," our first impulse is not to remember our own being forgiven, but instead to begin listing those who have done wrong to us, people who owe us, who are in the position of needing our forgiveness. Along with tax collectors and sinners, types who in the gospels so often end up coming to Jesus, asking for forgiveness, those listening to Jesus's story also include pharisees and scribes, a more problematic crowd. Can't you hear them, when they grumble among themselves: "This fellow welcomes sinners and eats with them." Whispering, shaking their heads, they are sure of their own righteousness and the wretchedness of others: "How is it that Jesus doesn't know how bad those tax collectors and their friends are? What kind of judge is he? We can tell you all the bad they have done; we know what they owe."

The older son enters Jesus's parable and makes the story about him. Surely the pharisees and the scribes nod in approval. You know, of course, that, in a way, this son is right? "For all these years, I have been working like a slave for you, and I have never disobeyed your command; yet you have never given me even a young goat so that I might celebrate with my friends." Ah, so much is here; isn't it? I don't know about the "working like a slave for you" stuff—this seems pretty far-fetched—but if the father had never given his son that goat, wouldn't you tend to agree, at least a little, with the son's complaint, with his pain? Especially after you heard the servant talk about that fatted calf for the younger brother? What kind of father is this, anyway? Doesn't he see that he is not being fair?

What kind of father, indeed. In order to answer this question, we might ask a few others: whose perspective in our story do we share? What kind of sons are these? What kind of children are we? How much better is one than the other? Go back and really listen to the younger son: "How many of my father's hired hands have bread enough to spare, but here I am dying of hunger!" In Jesus's parable, this son returns to his father not because of love or to make amends for what he has done. He returns because he is hungry. He understands only a part of his need. His perspective is not reliable. But the little he knows, the little he finally understands, somehow is enough. More than enough, because of who his father is. More than enough, thank our dear Lord, because that is how God's forgiveness works.

The older son is no better. He has lived with this loving father his whole life. I don't know what happened about the goat, but the older son's quickness with his silly calculus shows us he has been keeping careful count. He has a pretty good idea about what is owed to him. And he knows what he has suffered. We see that he is foolish and thick-headed. Looking into this son's angry eyes, what must his father think? What would you say to him, "Listen, kid, who do you think you are? Everything you have is from me." But instead, we hear what we could not have been expecting: "Son, you are always with me, and all that is mine is yours." "I have given you my life." "I love you."

The good father ends the parable. We are invited to open our hearts to love, forgiveness, new life, beyond anything we might have imagined: "We have to celebrate and rejoice, because this brother of yours was dead and has come to life; he was lost and has been found." When we realize the father in Jesus's parable acts out for us some part of what God's perspective must be, surely we are amazed, humbled, overwhelmed. Yet, our story ends somewhat abruptly. We don't know how the older brother responds. We don't know what happened next.

What do you want to happen?

— XIII —

Heading Toward Jerusalem

WE BEGIN TO SENSE a problem with the Incarnation: this becoming that has been fulfilled is one person. How does that one person bring along with him all of stubborn, suffering humanity? Once we have become uneasy, destabilized, will we move in the right direction? How does what is good prevail? Luke's repetitions illustrate only to open up wide into unsettling space. So that in chapter seven, we read about Jesus's healing the dying centurion's servant, then Jesus raises a widow's dead son, then we find John the Baptist in prison sending his disciples to Jesus.[1] The centurion's peculiar faith, his trusting on the basis of his personal experience of authority, that Jesus, if he wishes, will be able to heal his servant even though the servant is not in Jesus's presence, echoes, illustrates, then pushes further the stories Jesus has just told: "No good tree bears bad fruit, nor again does a bad tree bear good fruit" (6:43), and "I will show you what someone is like who comes to me, hears my words, and acts on them" (6:46). That centurion's good tree produces good fruit: his faith and compassion save his servant.

---

1. This sequence is unique to Luke. Matthew contains only the "good tree/good fruit; bad tree/bad fruit" saying and the healing of the centurion's servant. But a long interlude containing other sayings and Jesus's healing of a leper is in between them. John also briefly mentions Jesus's healing of the centurion's son. As he does so, he emphasizes Jesus's response, "Unless you see signs and wonders you will not believe" (John 4:48).

Heading Toward Jerusalem

Luke moves on. Jesus's healing reaches a widow crying over her dead son, a widow who does not seek out Jesus. Jesus's compassion for the widow (7:13) prompts his resurrecting her son. We have good fruit in abundance; we see acts of compassion, faith, and authority all come together to save and to heal. We know Jesus will resurrect those on the margins, a non-Jew's slave, a widow's son. Better, if they do not come to him, he will come to them. So we think we are finished.

But immediately, the disciples of John the Baptist enter. John is in prison. We readers know he is as good as dead. But John seems not to be worrying about himself. Instead, he wants to know who Jesus is. Jesus returns once more to the good tree/good fruit argument: "Go and tell John what you have seen and heard: the blind receive their sight, the lame walk, the lepers are cleansed, the deaf hear, the dead are raised, the poor have good news brought to them" (7:22). If the centurion acts out for us one reading of the good tree/good fruit parable and Jesus's raising the widow's son another, here Jesus overtly (or as overtly as Jesus ever does anything) claims he is that good tree. This matters, of course; we want to confirm who Jesus is. But it also seems oddly out of place. John and John's disciples ought to know enough about Jesus to know already what Jesus tells them. Then we remember John is in prison. John, too, is a good tree. He bears good fruit. If he is to hear Jesus's message as good news, surely that good news has relevance for his own situation? Luke places John's story within the context of Jesus's rewarding faith, Jesus's compassion, and his ability to raise the dead. But does that rewarding faith, compassion, resurrection reach to John?

John's fate stops us. We move, through essentially the same good tree/good fruit argument, from faith, compassion, miracle, to prison and defeat. We do not know exactly what to make of the defeat. Are we seeing the limits of an argument (Jesus says nothing about what happens to good trees?). We do not know where we are. Luke often destabilizes moments of great triumph. In chapter 9, the transfiguration leads directly to repeated failure, to an epileptic boy the disciples cannot heal, then to Jesus's prediction of his own betrayal and death, then to the disciples' ridiculous argument about who is the greatest among them, then to the disciples' trying to stop a healing in Jesus's name, then to the disciples wanting to call fire down from heaven upon a Samaritan village that has rejected Jesus. Luke gathers up these repeated failures.[2] They cast a growing shadow over Jesus's disciples, one that places verse 51 almost in chiaroscuro relief: "When the days drew near for him to be taken up, he set his face to go to Jerusalem."

---

2. While both Mark and Matthew contain some of these stories, neither of the other synoptic gospel writers contain them all, nor do they sequence the stories as Luke does. Mark is closer to Luke, yet his interruptions in the sequence as well as his moving forward, at the end, to other of Jesus's activities misses altogether Luke's punctuated "he set his face to go to Jerusalem."

— XIV —

Defeat

I talked to my Dad on Tuesday night. He told me that he was fitting into one of his favorite suits again (his treatments caused an unbelievable amount of swelling). He was feeling good. He said he looked great. Laughing at his perpetual confidence, regardless of what peeked out at him from the mirror, I found myself back on the beach in Florida. Once, while we were on a business trip to Boca Raton, David and I brought Pat, David's mother, with us; she loves tropical flowers, and she had never seen how beautiful Florida is. Because our hotel had prime beach space, my Dad asked us to meet him near the water. After unpacking, we made our way through the lobby, then walked down along the edge where the sand meets a boardwalk. Pat, covered up, maybe a little self-conscious, admired every plant in the hotel's formal garden, every bird, everything we saw. Out in the ocean, people were boogie boarding, then I heard my Dad yelling over the waves. He was coming in from the water. Wearing only a Speedo which his stomach almost covered over. So he looked, for a second, like he wasn't wearing anything. He smiled, laughed, came running up to greet us. I think because the possibility existed that he was naked, Pat understood that whatever she was wearing was just fine. It felt for all of us that my father's arms were open wide, wide enough to make us all comfortable, to let us all breathe deeply, laugh out loud.

Early Thursday morning, my brother called. Sleepy and out of sorts, I couldn't get a good grip on the phone. My brother kept trying to tell me that my father had died. But I didn't understand him. Then I just fell to the floor.

I had fallen once before because of my father. After his bypass, they let me into the recovery room. I suppose they did so because they thought I was vaguely medical. I hadn't eaten much for the whole of the day, and when I saw how grey my father's skin was, how small he looked on the table, how helpless, I passed out. A nurse caught me. I think they were more than a little annoyed. But my father laughed about it; we were in his room together just a few hours later.

The whole of our flight to Florida, I wanted to get off the plane. I think Henry and Alex sat on either side of me. Maybe not. I remember fiddling with some games for them. I also watched clouds out the window. So David must have held Alex. Henry was somehow next to him. Maybe.

I hate flying. I especially hate flying to Florida. Because the weather in the Gulf is so unpredictable. Awful really. When Henry was six, the two of us, because I had free tickets, flew to New Orleans to pick up a puppy. Two puppies; Jason wanted one. After we lost Jack, our dog we loved more than I can say, Henry read about all sorts of dogs on-line and decided that our family needed a Portuguese Water Dog. It made sense to me, but it turned out the nearest puppies were in New Orleans. So I went to New Orleans and picked up Frank, who mercilessly pestered everyone and ate rocks, clothes, toys, a couch. Frank's breeder, Robyn, became our friend and a year later told us she had another litter. Somehow it seemed like it would be a good idea to get a companion for Frank. And I had two free tickets. So Henry and I ended up on a plane to New Orleans.

We ate a great lunch, hung around with Robyn, and played with puppies. During lunch, we talked about how worried everyone in New Orleans was starting to get about the storm in the Gulf. We also talked a lot about *The Phantom Tollbooth* (we gave Milo his name at that lunch). We headed back to the airport with our puppy and Jason's. The puppies were so small; Henry was so small. I herded them all, carried both puppies in two sort of dog purses,

Defeat

and held onto Henry. Weather delayed our flight, then delayed it again. We had a horrible time getting into Houston. At the airport, people were running around, nervous; lots of flights were being cancelled. But I concentrated upon getting Henry and the puppies to our next gate. On the plane, our pilot warned us that it would be rough getting out of Houston. The flight from Houston to Austin takes a half an hour, maybe forty-five minutes. We were in the air two and a half hours because we couldn't get down. The storm in the Gulf, just south of Houston, was turning into Katrina that Friday night, and the winds of the storm were blowing directly between Austin and Houston. The sky outside the window was electric. The lights inside went out. We rocked, rolled; lightening flashed again and again. The puppies whimpered under the seat in front of us. I couldn't get to them. The stewardess sat in her jump seat with her head in her hands. She was crying. Henry threw up so much we used the five airsick bags I could find in our row of seats. People were moaning around us. I kept telling Henry everything was going to be okay. And I prayed. But I knew our lives had no more staying power than a snapped branch. I could not make out exactly how I had done such a foolish thing as to take Henry on this flight.

Thinking about my father's death is like falling headlong into that wind. I can't do it. I don't know how to do it.

A year later (or was it two; the sequence doesn't make sense to me), we were flying over the Gulf again. I can't tell you much about the funeral. But somehow, from my brother's phone call to our landing in Florida, my mind held open the possibility that what was going to happen, what had happened, could be avoided, could be fixed. That it was really terrible, but not the last word. That the plane would land safely.

Of course, it did. Someone, was it one of my brothers, was it the rabbi, was it David, thought we should go down in the line to look at my father in his casket. I had a hard time standing. I saw him through almost closed eyes for just a few seconds. I sat back down; we went through the rest of the service, and, after a few days, we came home.

The Gospel

I'll tell you what I do now, so many years later. Every so often, something will happen, I will hear *The Lion Sleeps Tonight* or the words "rice pudding," or I will feel my father's smile in the way I hold my lips when I mean something like, "Do you really think that is true?" or "I'll go along with you, but we both know that none of this makes any sense," and I will be brought to tears. And I find myself praying to God, telling God that God knows how wonderful my father was, how much he loved me, how much he protected me and took care of me, and that, no matter about theology and whatever my father did or thought that was wrong, God must love him and keep him and take care of him. And I plead with God. And I hope I will see my father again someday with his arms open wide.

— XV —

Crucifixion and All That Will Not Hold Together

WHAT DO WE DO in the place we find ourselves? Disciples tagging along, cheery, but repeatedly missing the point. An infinity of people who need to be healed. Hostility all around. John the Baptist dead. Where is the kingdom of God? One man, even though he is the Incarnation, can only go so far. People will not, do not change. Nor do the places they try to hold together. Then we read another repetition with a difference: "And it became, in the being filled completely, the days of his taking up, and he himself set the face to go into Jerusalem" (9:51). When we read in translations, "As the time approached for him to be taken up to heaven, Jesus resolutely set out for Jerusalem" (NIV), we miss Luke's once again forcing together "becoming" with "filling up." Christmas is over. But becoming and filling up are not. The days of his being taken up are becoming. Taken up on the cross. Taken up, victorious after the Resurrection, and ascension into heaven. Taken up by Luke's readers. Taken up by us. And as we collapse into this becoming "taken up" all of the tragedy and the victory surrounding the cross as well as its reach out of its story into our own, we find that what is becoming is somehow within a "filling completely." The moment Jesus chooses to walk toward Jerusalem, a moment in the midst of stupidity and failure, proves to be the moment when becoming is being filled completely. The kingdom of heaven breaks into the scene.

The Gospel

We come to straightforward prose; Jesus sets his face to Jerusalem, but we find this prose fully loaded, bursting at the seams.

Once Jesus is in Jerusalem, Luke chooses, in chapter 20, to repeat the situation of a group of questioners coming before Jesus.[1] Throughout the gospel of Luke, Jesus has used questions to open up his hearers' understandings, questions that penetrate and re-direct. Here, Jesus is the one being questioned: "By what authority are you doing these things?" (20:2). "Is it lawful for us to pay taxes to the emperor, or not?" (20:22). And, "In the resurrection, therefore, whose wife will the woman be?" (20:33). Each of Jesus's groups of questioners intends to trap Jesus. The repeated scene demonstrates how bad Jesus's situation truly is. People are coming at him from all directions, religious, political, personal, and they intend to finish him off. Yet, even here, Jesus responds with his own questions in order to break through, in order to open up. "Did the baptism of John come from heaven?" (20:4). "Show me a denarius. Whose head and whose title does it bear?" (20:24). "David thus calls him Lord; so how can he be his son?" (20:44). Each of these questions works like so many of Jesus's other questions. The kingdom of God bursts through from the inside. Answering these questions truthfully requires giving up a false structure. We readers know that Jesus wins all three arguments. We should be finished.

But, of course, we are not. Those present choose not to respond to Jesus. Luke's intense repetition of question-then-response-that-is-also-a-question ends, each time, in silence. Those questioning Jesus lose. But they choose not to notice. Trying to answer Jesus's answer-questions might have opened up for them glimpses into the kingdom of God, but really their own questions do not matter to them. Their structures matter; their power, their own religious

---

1. Matthew and Mark also contain this series, yet Matthew and Mark add to it a lawyer asking Jesus which is the greatest commandment (Matt 22:36; Mark 12:28). When Luke omits this question from his series, he omits Jesus's only positive response to this string of questioners: "You are not far from the kingdom of God" (Mark 12:34). In so doing, Luke repeats and emphasizes the inability of his questioners to respond to Jesus at the same time he intensifies the tension and hostility of the scene.

and political constructs. The old skins and the old wine. What can one man, even the Incarnation, do?

So much of Luke's gospel brings us to a choice. Letting go vs. holding on. Heaven vs. hell. And so many people wandering around Luke's landscapes, in parables and outside them, make the wrong choice. So that the landscape grows darker and darker. Jesus himself becomes silent. During his trial, almost the last thing Jesus says is, "If I tell you, you will not believe; and if I question you, you will not answer" (22:67–68). One man, even the Incarnation, will not make you budge. No more questions breaking in, opening up. No more stories. The last thing Luke's Jesus says during the sequence of his trial follows immediately after: "'But from now on the Son of Man will be seated at the right hand of the power of God.' All of them asked, 'Are you then the Son of God?' He said to them, 'You say that I am'" (22:69–70). Jesus's question-answers show who he is. Jesus here may be claiming that they know or ought to know the answers to their questions. Whether they want to acknowledge that they know these answers or not. Perhaps more seriously, he is claiming here that he will, from now on, be in the position of a judge over them. A silent judge. The scene in front of them, the structures they are depending upon and that they have created, will not hold. No matter what they think; no matter what they do. No matter what happens.

Jesus's arrest, trial, and crucifixion act out for us the absolute horror and, at the same time, the almost absurdist (almost, because "absurdist" cannot really be used in relation to that death on the cross) nature of our building up, relying on, defining ourselves by our own structures. We have a kind of power. And, too often, we use it. We believe that we can crucify Christ and hold onto the places we have made, the places we inhabit. How does the kingdom of God burst through to where we are? How do we move out of "this happened, then this, then this, and it got worse and worse"?

Praying in that garden, sweating as if he were bleeding, Jesus wrestles with the monstrosity of the place we have made, the place we want to hold onto. As he is being crucified, Jesus starts talking again. We feel the consistent pressure of God's love. "Father, forgive them; for they do not know what they are doing" (23:34). "Truly I tell you, today you will be with me in Paradise" (23:43). "Father, into your hands I commend my spirit" (23:46). Who are the "them" Jesus asks to be forgiven? Every one of us who does not know what he or she is doing. Jesus wants forgiveness for us; he says nothing to the thief who reviles him. The story is not about whether this thief is condemned. The story is about Jesus's promising to bring one condemned man to Paradise at the very last minute, the minute the kingdom of God opens up for him. Like the criminal next to Jesus, we need rescue from the world we find ourselves in, the world we have created, not to be reasoned out of it, but to be "taken up." We may think to ourselves, what about all the hell around us? What about . . . ? Then Luke's Jesus on the cross takes us back to his prayer in the garden: our hell may be real enough; the landscape, bleak; the world we are in may have neither justice nor mercy, but this is not the last word. "Into your hands . . ." God's will be done. Please, God's will be done. God's will will be done. God can be absolutely trusted, even when you are dying on a cross. God is up on the cross because he can be trusted. God looks down at us from the cross, all of us, and prays for our forgiveness.

We do not know what we do. We do not know very much. Luke's Easter depends upon our not knowing. For Luke, Easter is the kingdom of God repeatedly standing right in front of us and our not seeing it. Because we see our own things (things that are not even there, but that we have constructed never-the-less). Luke switches Mark's focus from the bewilderment and fear of the women at the tomb to the incredulity of the disciples when they hear the women tell their experience. Then to the two along the walk to Emmaus who do not recognize Jesus. But think they have the story right. Then to the gathered disciples who doubt what they see. Easter becomes Easter for all of them only after Jesus bursts through. Literally, standing in a room where he was not a moment before. Literally, "open[ing] their minds to understand the scriptures" (24:45), to understanding what has been written. Literally, inviting them to touch his wounded body. Their structures will not

Crucifixion and All That Will Not Hold Together

hold. Thank God. Their structures, our structures, were not working very well anyway. They could barely take care of the old; they were leaking all the time. New wine for new wineskins. A kingdom we never saw has been here all along.

Luke's gospel works to make us aware of where we are. And who is here. If we could only see this; if we could be taken up in the reverberation; if we could recognize and be thankful for the flow of heaven into our lives . . . Too often, we feel we cannot get out of our structures. Or we just don't want to. We find ourselves trying to hold onto, trying to maintain the time we think we know. But this time is just an in-between time. A time waiting for the "having been fulfilled" to break through "it came to pass" and to transform it, to bring us into the becoming kingdom of God. As we read the gospel of Luke, we find challenge rising up out of our comfort, our lesson, the stable ground we have perched ourselves upon. Then the moment we can take it no longer, we find comfort reaching up out of the challenge. This movement, as it undoes structure, is essential to the structure of Luke's gospel. As we read, Luke's text repeats, re-directs, opens up, placing us in a state of necessary disequilibrium. Necessary for Easter, for our letting the kingdom in.

How Acts Means

— XVI —

Wittgenstein and My Grandmother

My grandmother butters meat sandwiches. Ham, turkey, bologna, even tuna fish all start between two slices of bread smeared with margarine. Other things end up on the bread as well. Sometimes tomatoes, pickles, a little cheese. But the margarine is always there.

When my grandfather took me fishing, we would quietly, without naming the problem to each other, try to work around these sandwiches.[1] As Nana pulled out the bread, I might say, "I can make the sandwiches, if you'd like." Or even, "You know, I don't know how much I like butter with ham." Nana, shaking her head against my help, would direct me to dirty dishes. She was (and pretty much still is) sure of herself. "Of course, you like butter with ham. That's how sandwiches are made." Once she made such a pronouncement, Grandpa would say, "We'll be glad to eat when it's hot tomorrow," and he would disappear. On our fishing days, we left at four in the morning, so, at one, when we took a break, we were hungry. I dreaded those sandwiches. But Grandpa would uncover from underneath an old army blanket in the back of his Jeep a big bakery box full of iced brownies and peanut butter cookies. They were his secret insurance. During the afternoon, we mostly ate brownies and drank orange soda pop while neither of

---

1. After her divorce, Nana married a wonderful man who claimed all of us as his family.

us officially noticed the other feeding ham and tuna and bologna and cheese to the ducks.

Permeable boundaries. Words that are on the edge of something that then turn on you and try to edge you in. We enter into the game of language and win, because, after all, sticks and stones can break your bones . . . , but we also lose. Wittgenstein would have liked my grandmother, but my grandmother would not like Wittgenstein. Or at least what some of his words represent. She probably would have felt sorry for the man. All that suspect Viennese aristocracy, the tutors, the hyper-formal family life, the three brothers who killed themselves. When you read about Wittgenstein's life maybe the worst part is finding out what a demanding, even cruel teacher he was. But, of course, the more you read, the more his failings make sense. Given his circumstances. What doesn't altogether make sense and what is, for me, the most beautiful thing about his life, about any life really, are the epiphanies, the break-outs. My grandmother, collapsed on the floor of her bedroom, praying, discovering God as her first husband abandoned her. Wittgenstein giving up his fortune, a German, serving incognito as a hospital orderly in war-torn London, spending time hanging in and about monasteries.

As I think about it, my grandmother most likely would find Wittgenstein extremely disagreeable because she would sense that he did not exactly believe in what most of us mean by Truth. I wonder if she met him, if she would give him credit for trying to get near truth even so. Or at least for trying to describe some of its boundaries. I don't know. He might have liked his sandwiches buttered and that would throw the whole business in the opposite direction.

As my father began to live with my being a Christian, he didn't say a lot about it, but early on, he told me that, given who I was (and I think he meant this as a compliment), my faith would not last. "There are all those manuscripts, and they don't match." I didn't know what my father was talking about. "All the manuscripts, the ones the Christians use, they say different things; they are not the same." I still didn't know what my father was talking about. I think he had done some reading. "Greek. Their bible is written in very old Greek. And it has a lot of writers. And the pieces of it contradict each other. And what is translated doesn't match all the old manuscripts because it can't, because they don't match." I'm afraid I didn't recognize the love that went into his argument. Instead, it just felt like somehow I had lost. I told him I would look into it. And I did. I signed up for New Testament Greek the next semester.

It turns out, in Greek classes, you don't get to the manuscripts for a really long time. But you do get to something else, almost right away. You get to be somewhere you have never been. Struggling through declensions, I started to see some of what a declined language can do. For one thing, because of word endings, Greek sentences do not have to be our linear, listening for the subject sort of affairs. In Greek, word order matters, but in an entirely different way: The verb to emphasize first you may put it if you would like. Moving words around in a sentence, mirroring, apposition, alliterating, all of these things we do, but (maybe) declined Greek allows ancient Greek writers to do these things a little better. To construct sentences that poke out at you and draw you in and work like puzzles and make the world they describe seem so very loaded. I fell in love. What would the precision and the freedom in this kind of writing allow you to see in the world? What would it be like to listen in conversation all the way to ends of words instead of jumping from beginning to beginning?

Further and further into my studies, my Dad's manuscript problem did not hold up. Lots of little differences, genitives for datives, plurals mixed with singulars, but hardly any substantial ones. In all those manuscripts. My father remained skeptical, but one day he handed me a t-shirt he brought back from Greece. Because I could translate the Greek written across the front of the t-shirt (the beginning of the Odyssey), he seemed very pleased. With me and with himself. Because both he and I knew how much of Dad was in my trying to learn Greek. The t-shirt, almost twenty years old now, is still in my closet. And when I wear it, which is not too often because I want it to last forever, I notice people trying to make out what is written on it. More than once, wearing that t-shirt, I have been in a store or a parking lot or in line, and a stranger says something like, "What is that? What does it say?" We then spend a few minutes together on our own journey. Even if, looking upside down, I can't translate perfectly what is written (looking head on, I also can't translate perfectly—it is poetry, after all), more often than not, we make a connection. Sometimes I hear a better translation than I could have imagined. Or a story about how wonderful it was the first time someone read Homer.

Reading is like that. It opens wide worlds and worlds. And maybe faith is the best kind of reading. Doors, windows flung open. First, we peek out, then we stand for a while amazed, then we may even climb or run through because we want to see more and more of what is there. That moment when you get a glimpse of a part of something that you want to follow and follow to find out what it is. The night before every first day of school, I have always had a hard time sleeping. If I lay down worried because someone has told me one too many times about where I am supposed to go to catch the bus and how important it is to be there on time (what would happen if I missed the bus?), more often than not, I would find myself at two, then three in the morning, walking around my room, thinking about all that I was on the edge of, all that I was about to learn.

Before the first day of first grade, I sat in my bed looking out over the Bay of Naples at Mount Vesuvius in the distance. I was five years old; I knew that danger is real. We had been to Pompeii and had seen the shapes of bodies trapped in the hardened ash, some of them holding onto one another forever. But then there was that beautiful, sleepy mountain, stars shining down on it, and the light on the water between us. Would I learn all that I wanted to know? And how would I be able to do that? What was about to happen to me? I put my clothes on; it must have been somewhere between four and five. I sat and looked out my window. And thought about all the things that might come next. Which word would follow, which word to follow? When my father came in to wake me up, I was dressed, with my shoes and socks on, sitting on the edge of my bed, wondering if I was ready for the day to start.

— XVII —

Shipwreck

MORE GREEK. AGAIN, SKIP this if you'd like. I don't know quite how else to explain what odd things happen when you hear every word. Or at least try to.

"*Kai diasothentes*" ("*having been saved through,*" saved from the storm, passive—who has done the saving?) "*then we knew.*" Makes a certain sense, having been saved through (a storm), we know something: "*hoti Melita hey nasos kaleitai.*" After all the translation, we actually don't know much, just that "*the island is called Malta.*" Wait. "We *knew.*" Immediately before this, "*they*" were in a shipwreck (Acts 27). Suddenly, Luke has, we have made a sea-change. Now, "*we*" are knowing things. "*We*" are among the survivors. Luke has come out into the open. He is telling a story he is part of.

"*Hoi te barbaroi*" (the "*barbaros,*" an ominous word for native people; "barbarians," even worse) "*offered not the having happened/ usual* (usual? What is usual for barbarians?) *love for fellow people to us. For having kindled/started a fire, they received all of us on account of the coming rain and the cold.*" What a lovely picture. All this unexpected care from barbarians. If we could just stop here.

But no. Nothing stands still. So that "*echidna*" has to show up. "*But, Paul, having gathered up a large number of sticks and having laid [them] upon the fire,*" (for a second, we are all in this together) "*echidna,*" "*a viper, venomous snake* (and, I saw the picture, much later, the name for a small spiny anteater in Australia) *came out from the heat, taking hold of his hand."* Unintended consequence. Unexpected disaster. Again. Shipwreck. Rescue. Warmth. Viper. *"And as the barbarians saw the dangerous animal hanging from his hand,"* (freeze frame: what would I do?) *"they were saying to one another,"* "pantas," "certainly" (at this point, what, in fact, is certain?), *"a murderer is this man, having been brought safely through out of the sea, Justice does not permit to live."* (Not an altogether unreasonable supposition. Would I say this?)

Another turn. *"Then, on the other hand, having shaken off the dangerous animal into the fire, he suffered nothing evil. But they were waiting/expecting/looking for him to be about to burn with fever or fall down suddenly dead."* Of course, they were. Things ought to make sense. *"But they, having waited/expected/looked for a while and seeing nothing out of place becoming unto him,"* "Metabalomenoi," "turning, throwing around, changing their minds"—this is the word for the passage—*"they were saying him to be a god."*

— XVIII —

How Things Are In Acts

IN ACTS, THINGS ARE slippery. Standing back, we might think we can name Luke's intention. He means to be as comprehensive as possible, a good historian. But, deep in the writing, I start to go under. Luke twists, turns, moves piece by piece, moment by moment. I try to read on and watch amazed as Luke quietly and carefully creates a landscape, maybe even a whole world, not by building an argument or by following a biographical line, but by telling, telling everything he can. Maybe that's why Wittgenstein so often hovers around when I read Acts. I leads to Ia then to Ib and obviously next to II, but how? Peter, Paul, Luke, all of us, are going somewhere. Each step is connected. But where? What sense does it make?

As he collects his (astounding) information, Luke writes an account, several accounts, maybe a very long letter, a history, histories, an invitation, a . . . . What coalesces, Acts, describes with precision and care a world that none of its readers might quite recognize, but one, as it develops before us, Luke insists is the world that is. Luke is deep in this world; he is not trying to explain it. I probably better defend the Wittgenstein connection. Wittgenstein starts his own enterprise with a peculiar sequence:

I. The world is everything that is the case.

I.I. The world is the totality of facts, not of things.

I.II. The world is determined by the facts, and by these being *all* the facts.

How Acts Means

> I.I2. For the totality of facts determines both what is the case, and also all that is not the case.[1]

For me, Acts is more a piling up of Wittgensteinian facts than a simpler empirical piling up of things. Luke gives us the facts right in front of him, the facts he can collect, and Acts pictures Luke's world, "the world," "the case," so that Theophilus, so that anybody reading Acts, might see it.

Because Luke focuses on "facts" and not just on "things," how Acts comes together, to the extent that it does and even to the extent that it does not come together, has meaning in itself, even perhaps suggests a kind of fundamental meaning of and in Acts. In his gospel, Luke is caught up in Jesus's many proclamations that the kingdom of heaven is here. Once Jesus leaves the scene, Luke, all the apostles, disciples, early Christians, are left with here where the kingdom of heaven just was. If the miracles in Acts suggest that such a kingdom keeps popping out again, what Luke narrates in Acts is his discovery/re-discovery of this kingdom, or his attempts to do so, fact by fact. Seeing the world that Luke finds as he brings together Acts, we receive from Acts an invitation to try to make it out, to embrace it, to recognize in Luke's world the very world in which we ourselves live.

To see the world in Acts, it is useful to revisit the world in the gospel of Luke. Confident metaphors dominate the world of the gospel. Opening the gospel, extensive passages of Old Testament prophesy, full of pictures of the coming kingdom, promise that the baby Jesus will be, for example, "a horn of salvation" (1:69), "the rising sun" (1:78), "a light for revelation to the Gentiles" (2:32), and "a sword" that will "pierce" his mother's soul (2:35). To the ears of those who heard it, Jesus's earliest conversation reported in Luke is based in metaphor, "Didn't you know I had to be in my Father's house?" (2:49). Jesus calls the first disciples with a metaphor: "Don't be afraid; from now on you will fish for people" (5:10). The many parables in Luke, occupying whole sequences of chapters, are often extended metaphors. Metaphors frame, inform

---

1. Ludwig Wittgenstein, *Tractatus Logico-Philosophicus,* trans. C. K. Ogden (Boston: Routledge & Kegan Paul, 1983), 31.

and enliven Jesus's sermons themselves: "Give, and it will be given to you. A good measure, pressed down, shaken together and running over, will be poured in your lap" (6:38). Or, "No good tree bears bad fruit, nor does a bad tree bear good fruit. Each tree is recognized by its own fruit . . . . The good man brings good things out of the good stored up in his heart, and the evil man brings evil things out of the evil stored up in his heart" (6:43–44a, 45). Indeed, on his way to the cross, Jesus continues to speak in metaphor, "For if people do these things when the tree is green, what will happen when it is dry?" (23:31).

To live then, in the gospel of Luke, is to live in metaphor. What does this mean and what does it do to someone absorbing a metaphor? Making comparisons between unlike things and so insisting upon these comparisons that you choose to leave out any bridge ("like" or "as," for instance) back to the ground from which you started places the person accepting the metaphor firmly in your world. The very dissimilarity upon which metaphor depends prevents an easy exit because accepting the given comparison destabilizes the original position of the hearer. Trying to work out the metaphoric vision, the hearer is caught. "You can be fishers of people. Think about it. See it." "You want to be a good tree. Who would want to be a bad?" Of course, one can imagine the stubborn response, "No, I will not catch anybody," or "I am not a tree at all." Not everyone who hears will understand or see (how many times and in how many ways do we read this throughout the gospel?). The point is that once you do begin to admit the comparison, once it gets under your skin, you find yourself in a different world than the place you started. In the world as seen by someone else, in the gospel of Luke, the world as Luke tells us that Jesus sees.

What is it like to be in this world? In Luke, a curious thing begins to happen to metaphors as figures of speech. When the child Jesus says in the temple that he is in his Father's house, the people hearing this, perhaps excluding Mary and Joseph, if Joseph is there, may think something like, "I understand this metaphor. We are all metaphorically children of God. The temple is where we worship God. So when any of us are in the temple, we are in our

Father's house." But we, as we immerse ourselves in Luke's gospel, may hear Jesus make a different claim; we may hear a more specific Father-Son relationship. As Christians, we start to feel that the pressure point of the comparison is in its base not in its vision; that is, what is more real is what started out to be the imaginary leg of the comparison. We find this in Luke's straight narrative, for example: "So [Jesus] bent over her and rebuked the fever and it left her" (4:39). Told to go away, the fever went. What does this mean? Stumbling along after Jesus, the disciples more and more wonder about what exactly it is that they are seeing: "In fear and amazement they asked one another, 'Who is this? He commands even the winds and the water, and they obey him'" (8:25). By the time we arrive at the Last Supper and Jesus tells us, "This is my body given for you"; "This cup is the new covenant in my blood, which is poured out for you" (22:19, 20), those of us who know the rest of the story are with the disciples. We know this sounds like metaphorical language, but that it is something different. The visionary leg of the comparison seems to be all that is left. Luke's relentless "kingdom of heaven/God" language insists "the kingdom of God has come to you" (11:20). What begins as a vision, what metaphor allows, ends as reality; the scaffold of metaphor disappears.

In Acts, the ground beneath us shifts. Shaky itself, this ground unsettles metaphor, does not allow for it; indeed, given the preponderance of metaphor in Luke, the relative absence of metaphor in Acts may be one of its most remarkable features. When he writes largely without metaphor, what is Luke telling his readers about the world in Acts? What sort of a place is it? In Acts 28:1–6, surviving a shipwreck, Paul, Luke (we are in one of the "we" passages), and the rest of the ship's company find themselves bedraggled on the shore of Malta.[2] Within two verses, the landscape changes

2. Here it is again, if this is helpful: (1) And then having been safe through/having come safe through, we came to know that the island is called Malta. (2) And the barbarians were offering not the normal love of mankind for us for, starting a fire, they received us all on account of the rain coming on and on account of the cold. (3) But Paul having gathered up some large number of sticks and having laid them upon the fire, a viper, having come out from the heat, took hold of his hand. (4) And when the barbarians saw the beast hanging

three times: "having been safe through/having come safe through," the shipwreck is over. On land again, safe, better, on recognizable land, Malta, we are at the end of a crisis. But then *hoi barbaroi*, the barbarians, appear. "Barbarians," whatever else they are, people not like yourself and people with whom you may not be able to speak, contain within themselves potential for danger. We read that they "offer not the normal love of mankind for us." Maybe, for a second, we miss Luke's understatement and think that these barbarians could do something harmful? But our worry is almost immediately overturned. These unintelligible people start a fire and receive "us." Luke's readers may hear the civilized/uncivilized slur underpinning *barbaros* and, at the same time, witness the highly civilized behavior, offering kindness beyond normal expectation, of the barbarians. We see and then we see again, but we are not sure about what we are looking at. Without much imaginative effort, we may find we are in a somewhat familiar shipwrecked boat. Like Paul, Luke, and probably the barbarians, we make our way through the landscape of Acts (and how many other places?) asking ourselves (again and again) where exactly are we? And with whom? Have we come safe through?

---

from his hand, to each other they were saying—by all means a murderer is this man who, having been safe through the sea, Justice did not permit to live. (5) Then he, having shook off the beast into the fire, he suffered nothing evil. (6) But they were waiting for him to be about to burn with fever or fall down suddenly dead. But after a long while, waiting for and seeing nothing out of place happening to him, having changed their minds, they were saying he was a god.

— IXX —

Horse Stories

DAVID AND I WERE there when Bryce was born. I had been doing urine tests on Pippi, his mother, so we knew she was going to give birth within a twelve hour window. We drove the horse trailer next to the barn so we could take her to the vet, if we needed. Curious, our other horses ran around and around the trailer. We went into the paddock to keep Pippi calm. Because I had read a story online about a young horse drowning in a water trough, we put Pippi's trough up on cement blocks. Then we wandered around the pasture, trying to find more problems. Mark came to see if Pippi's baby had arrived. While David and Mark talked together at the barn, I ran to the house to check on Henry and Alex and to make something to eat. As I was loading up our pickup with the lawn chairs we were going to sleep in, I saw waves and waves of dust way up at the barn swirling around the horse trailer. Sure that Pippi's baby was coming, I jumped in the truck. When I got to the top of the hill, David and Mark were standing next to the horse trailer. David was holding Jesse, one of our oldest horses. Jesse's leg was bleeding, and it looked distorted. At some point in the whirl of horses, Jesse had tried to jump over the connection between the trailer and the truck that was pulling it and had got caught in the chains. Although Jesse had lain very still as David and Mark worked to get him out, the torque of falling while he was caught in the chain seemed to have broken his leg.

Horse Stories

Jesse saved my life once. Back, when I boarded him at Alida's, Jesse came down with a virus which caused a slight fever and runny nose. I went to check on him. Because it was a Sunday afternoon and I had the time, I brought Jack with me. No one was at the barn. Throwing a towel over my shoulder, I took a halter, a bag of carrots and Jack on a leash into the pasture where Jesse was grazing in the back with nine or ten other horses. It was a beautiful day; five months pregnant with Henry, I was so happy. When Jack and I were about half way across the field, all the horses suddenly started to run toward us. I thought someone must be up at the barn blowing a whistle and turned around to see, but no one was there. By the time I turned back around to find Jesse, all the horses in the pasture were on us and began to circle madly. Jack was a 110 pound black dog who often was mistaken for a wolf. I had never thought about it, but Alida's dogs, who were always in the barn, mostly stayed out of the pasture. Realizing what I had done, I started frantically yelling all the horse's names, "Lady. Fina. Gabe. Wyatt." Dirt and dust lashed around us. The circle got tighter, and Jack put himself between my legs. I threw carrots. I whipped the towel and the halter in the air. When I ran out of carrots, I threw clods of dirt. Two of the lead geldings reached down and grabbed tufts of Jack's hair. I began crying, praying, all at the same time. I was still shouting.

How much planning is enough? And whose? How do we manage? I was pretty sure that when the horses wanted to, they would turn in and start to kick. Firecloud and Wyatt were running around us with their hinds curved toward us. Jack whimpered and winced as his hair flew by. We heard some new shrill noise. Part of the circle around us elongated. Then horses were moving against the circle, in every direction, and away from us. Jesse, who I had not seen, was kicking the heck out of Wyatt. Jack and I found a space and ran. We heard Firecloud squealing. Jesse was chasing him across the pasture. We dove underneath a fence. The horses were running every which way, while Jesse pushed first Firecloud then Wyatt back and back. The two of them finally ran as hard as they could away from Jesse. And an amazing thing happened. (Or another amazing thing. Or another.) Jesse ran across the pasture to the fence where Jack and I were standing. He stood next to us. As I thanked him again and again, Jesse reached over the fence and touched his nose to Jack's head. I'm not sure how long the three of us stood there.

Jesse ran back to where Firecloud was. And then another amazing thing happened. Peri, Alida's horse who was Jesse's best friend, ran up to us at the fence and walked alongside us as we went back to the barn. Meaning to take care of Jesse, I found myself being saved by him. And watched over by his friend. What was Jesse thinking? About what was happening? About me? We believe that we are in one story, that we master the places we find ourselves, managing things, perhaps doing what is right, but we find out we are in another and another story, and we are not very often the heroes. What was Jesse thinking? I know we were friends. Somehow he had come to love me. The gift of that love changed so many sequences, put new stories there for me and put them in motion.

Jesse didn't die the day Bryce was born. The vet came. After all sorts of poking and prodding, she decided that probably his leg was just badly sprained, bruised; a mess, but not a fatal mess. When he did die, of old age, after years of retirement next to Peri in our own pasture, I was there. Henry, David, Alex, all of us, lost more than a dear friend. We lost one of us.

Driving with his tennis coach to Waco the week after Jesse died, Henry told her about Jesse. Somehow or another he used Jesse's racehorse name, Inevitable Choice. The coach grabbed at her phone and called her sister-in-law. Henry didn't know what was happening. The next twenty minutes were pretty confusing, but it turns out that Jeanne, the sister-in-law, owned Jesse early in his life, right after his racing days, when he was four or five, after he had broken a leg on the track. Jesse survived complicated surgery; Jeanne hand-walked him for several months. Jesse recovered slowly. Having just graduated from law school, Jeanne was planning, with her mother, to work a bit, settle into land, train horses, a life they had talked and talked about, but her mother died suddenly of a heart attack. Jesse was a gorgeous horse, a big bay with

Horse Stories

black socks and a commanding presence. Aware of Jeanne's circumstance, the vet who had done Jesse's surgery convinced Jeanne to sell Jesse. While the vet claimed he was going to keep him for his own, he, in fact, sold him almost immediately to a hunter-jumper barn, a disaster for Jesse because of the pin in his leg. He was most likely in pain for a few years and was passed from place to place. Finally, when he was eight, Jesse ended up at a slaughterhouse.

With Alida's help, a teen-aged girl rescued Jesse, and, not knowing about his leg, started him in jumping competitions. Jeanne was judging a steeplechase when Jesse ran by. She immediately recognized him, pulled him off the course, asked the rider what she thought she was doing, and found out Jesse had been at the slaughterhouse. She wanted him back, but the girl was discombobulated by her forcefulness and did not trust Jeanne. Two months later, Jesse's new family was transferred to Germany. Not knowing about Jeanne, Alida talked me into taking him. No one told Jeanne what had happened. Heartsick, Jeanne lost track of Jesse, though she pieced together some of what I have told you. All those years later, she felt she had found him again. She jumped in her car, drove to Waco, and sat with me at the tennis tournament. And cried and cried. She told me that she had prayed for Jesse every day since she lost track of him, that she had felt such guilt about the selling him, that she, so many years later, still lost sleep because she didn't know what had happened to him.

I sent her lots pictures.

Bryce was born the day after we thought Jesse broke his leg. At about one in the morning, Pippi's labor began. We saw two front feet, turned right, and a head in the right place. And I said a prayer thanking God because I knew everything was okay. But, as her labor went on and on, I started timing where we were. I couldn't believe that we were in trouble. We called our neighbor, also a vet, to ask what she thought. It was almost two in the morning. And she came over right away. She said Bryce was too big, but then she managed to pull Bryce out of his mother. We watched as he quickly got to his feet. And we celebrated, thanked God; our wonderful neighbor went home. Not able to sleep, David and I sat in the back of the truck. Bryce sauntered around the paddock. Then, all of a sudden, he began to trot. It was like a dream, magnificent. We came to the fence to watch him just in time for him to make it to the water trough, somehow position his legs up on the cedar blocks we had put there earlier for his protection, and fall head first into the water. I started running. He was thrashing about, impossibly hard to hold, but we fished him out of the trough. And took him as far away from it as we could. And fell down exhausted, not sure what we were going to do with the trough. Or what might happen next.

— XX —

The Slipperiness Of Meaning

ON MALTA, IT TURNS out that Paul and his companions are among compassionate, open people (but, as we know because by chapter 28 we are late in Acts, it could have gone the other way). Verses 3–6 suggest that these "barbarians" themselves have a problem similar to that of the shipwrecked group. A viper comes out of heat and fastens itself to Paul so that Luke sees the snake hanging from Paul's hand. Separate from the immediate crisis, this situation, if it occurred in some other story, poem, painting, movie, dream would present the very stuff of metaphors: the snake is a devil; the snake connected to Paul is a judgment—the snake is Paul's sinfulness coming back to bite him; the snake is random evil; the snake is whatever Freud says it is; the snake is . . . . Of course, the residents of Malta try to make meaning out of a viper hanging from the hand of a shipwreck survivor. And the meaning they make is reasonable: Paul is guilty of something so serious that Justice will not allow him to survive with the others who were on the boat. Wicked people (eventually) meet their appropriate fates. This may be so or maybe we should just hope it is so or maybe we should hope it is not so. But the main point of what happens is that straining for meaning, Luke's barbarians miss the mark. The viper is a fact, but in what world?

Paul shakes the snake off into the fire, and they wait. Specifically, they wait for something bad to happen to him. Because they know how to read the signs, they have taken the metaphoric leap and are on the other side. When nothing happens to him, they are not troubled. Instead, they contextualize what they've seen, add in the last part, and make a better metaphor, one of a very similar quality to those metaphors in the gospel of Luke in which the compared collapses into the comparison: Paul is a god. When post-modern semiotic theorists try to describe language games, to describe structures that determine outcomes, they could not have a better model than Acts 28:1–6. Yet, this story itself is in a context, and that context calls into question the interpretative strategies of the people who find Paul and his friends. Luke nestles this story within the "not the normal love of mankind" displayed by his barbarians who, as the story progresses, receive healing from Paul and considerably help the shipwreck victims throughout the winter and on their way to Rome. Luke does not seem to be calling into questions these people themselves; indeed, he remembers them with great fondness. But the metaphoric habit of mind, the jumping as quickly as one can to a visionary, but also consistent, stable place, does not hold. The facts, leading to something, defy the metaphors. What was that snake?

For that matter, in Acts, what is that prison? Or that window? Or a belt? Or a handkerchief? Or an apron? Or a shadow? Or a shipwreck? Or a trial? Or a . . . ? A prison is a place where prisoners are kept. And a prison is a description of a condition from which Peter, Paul (all of us?) need to be free. That window is an opening marking a boundary where a young man can fall outside; that window may mark a threshold between believers and unbelievers. The belt is a strap that holds up Agabus' pants; the belt is a strap that indicates Paul will be bound. Paul uses handkerchiefs and aprons in his work. The healing work of Paul happens through handkerchiefs and aprons. Peter casts a shadow. Peter's shadow casts out illness. A shipwreck ends a journey, takes the ship's travelers off-course. A shipwreck is and is not a catastrophe and may bring us to a place we need to be. A trial determines innocence and guilt. Paul's trial is not a trial, yet Paul experiences trial after trial. These words, these and many other moments in Acts like them, all elude metaphor; they do not bring us to certain visionary reality,

The Slipperiness Of Meaning

yet each of them, with very little effort, becomes figurative. If we to whom Acts is given cannot get to the kingdom by seeing it with Jesus, we get somewhere in Acts by pressing on the facts we have and finding what is contiguous to them. Our movement through Acts is metonymic, part for whole, fact abutting thing. Indeed, to rush through a reading of Acts is to feel like parts are strewn all around you. Because we know what prisons, windows, belts, handkerchiefs are, it is easy to miss the metonyms. Metonyms work best when you consider them slowly, when you respect tentative vision, the work in progress.

— XXI —

Alex Krutov

When we saw Alex Krutov last week, he seemed tired. Almost talking to himself, he kept repeating, "God works in mysterious ways." During the winter, the Harbor lost some big donors. Hoping to make up the difference before returning to Russia in the summer, Alex had been scrambling across the U.S. In his precise English that moves up and down just enough to recall maybe a vampire, maybe the Swedish Chef, he traced for us driving back and forth across Texas from Houston to San Antonio, Austin, Dallas, Austin, San Antonio, Abilene, somewhere close to Amarillo, then back to Houston. As we ate dinner, we heard about orphans across Russia, single mothers, orphans themselves, in the Harbor's mothering program so that they might hold onto their children, other aged-out orphans whom the Harbor collects and brings together as a family for a few years, providing them with love, structure, and training, maybe in carpentry, I.T., cooking, doing some college prep, then all of the others Alex wanted to reach, the countless drug addicts, prostitutes, petty criminals, who "graduate" from state-run orphanages with "orphan" stamped across their identification papers, that stamp forecasting their opportunities, directing them towards government-run housing projects on the farthest edges of big cities, without employment, without hope.

Alex himself was such a graduate. Five years after aging-out of his orphanage, most of his friends were in prison, were about to go to prison, were addicts, or were dead. They were statistically the norm. Growing up in state care meant for Alex having little to no connection with loving adults. It meant being beaten, knowing children who disappeared, who died. Alex is just a wisp of a person. He has serious food issues because of institutional food and because of childhood illnesses. For a brief period, he was adopted out to a family where he was abused. Twelve years old, he ran away to the center of St. Petersburg and spent a Russian winter living in a cardboard box. He was returned to the orphanage more dead than alive.

When Alex tells his story, it feels like you are reading something. A story you want to let you go, you want to get to the end of. I met Alex through reading. Henry was two or three, and I was about as happy as it is possible to be. One morning, I picked up a *Washington Post*, and saw a large photo featuring the frightened face of a straight-jacketed baby lying in a row with other straight-jacketed babies. The article described conditions in Russian Orphanages for the Disabled. In Russia, children with everything from severe hydrocephalus to speech impediments to club foot are separated from other orphans and taken to institutions that are often in more disrepair, more understaffed, understocked, hidden than even the "normal" orphanages like the one that housed Alex. Children classified as disabled remain their entire lives wards of the state. Anecdotally, I know that many of these children do not reach adulthood.

I found myself not able to stop thinking about this article, even praying that I would not stop thinking about it. Around this time, I heard a medical missionary speak about his work in central America and discovered that the Episcopal church had a regional medical missions committee. Asking them if I could present at their next meeting, I brought to Houston my dog-eared copy of the *Washington Post* along with other bits of information I had collected about orphanages for the disabled in Russia. The whole business was unnecessarily formal. The committee sat in a line at a table, and I sat in front of them. I did not expect their questions and comments: "What level are these children? Do they understand where they are?" "Wouldn't our money be of better use helping higher functioning children?" "We cannot change their situation so what help can we offer?" I suppose, in hindsight, at least the last of these rose up out of reasoned concern and a dutiful wish to get the most for the money the committee oversaw. The committee chose not to pursue Russian orphanages for the disabled as a mission area.

As I was walking to my car, one of the committee members came up to me. He seemed embarrassed by what had just happened. "I don't know if this will help," he mumbled, "but there is a priest, Mark Browne, in Connecticut who visits Russian orphanages." He shook my hand and gave me a piece of paper with a number written across it.

When I called him, Mark would not stop talking. He had taken several groups to Russia who wanted to work with orphans. They spent some of their time in summer camps for orphans that originally had been intended as Communist propaganda camps (Alex Krutov remembers these camps as a few weeks of opportunity to eat fresh vegetables). Mark's stories were sobering. During his last trip, a child had fallen down onto a high voltage transmission line and had died. Yet, Mark spoke about his time in Russia with remarkable enthusiasm. When I asked him about orphanages for the disabled, he started laughing. I wasn't sure what to make of this. The last group who had traveled with him to Russia included a family from the Austin area. Because they had disabled twins, they were curious when they met no disabled orphans. Through some fairly complicated maneuvers, they found Pavlosk, the St. Petersburg area home for such children. Their persistence and kindness along with their own story gained them an afternoon's entrance into Pavlosk. They found a few staff members trying to take care of what seemed like over a hundred children, some of them infants, many of them with serious special needs. The medicine and supply room was mostly empty. Staff members seemed touched by Lewis and Linda, by how the two of them behaved with the children. At the end of their time together, Lewis and Linda were invited to return. Then they came home to Texas. They did not know what they were going to do next. From Connecticut, Mark, confident, oddly bubbly, connected me to Lewis and Linda who live just down the road.

Through our churches and friends, we invited anyone interested in helping Russian orphans to my house to talk. We collected people who had been to Russia with Mark Browne, a friend who had an adopted Russian two year old, a few people (one of them being Melissa who has become one of my dearest friends) simply moved like I was by the story of these orphans. We met. We talked. We met again. And we started figuring things out. During the next several years, some of us (not me) traveled to Russia many times. We supplied Pavlosk with over-the-counter medications, first aid supplies, of course toys, blankets, books; the lists grew and grew. We gained access to a second, then a third orphanage for the handicapped, and we arranged for the installation of necessary sump pumps and other plumbing, even a playground. In Russia, disabled orphans are officially not candidates for adoption, but Lewis and Linda were able to adopt Lanie, a young woman with a variety of congenital abnormalities who was about to age into permanent institutionalization. As our group went into this and then into that orphanage, we began to meet others, Germans, Dutch, some Russians, all of whom felt called to sort out the mess of orphanages for the disabled in Russia. That mess is still being sorted out; Russian policy on foreign help has hardened considerably, and yet I don't think you would recognize Pavlosk as the same place Lewis and Linda first visited. Somehow, the situation is, in fact, better. With a lot more better still needed.

Linda and Lewis met Alex Krutov in Russia and saw what he was trying to do at the Harbor. We became part of his American circle, and he visits us once or twice a year. We all, especially our Alex, love him. How many other people are able to appreciate appropriately how marvelous it is that our eleven year old identified, in the school-wide geography bee (David and I were glued to our seats), Astana as the capital of Kazakhstan? Tracing Alex's Krutov's peculiar geography presents a different sort of difficulty. His borders are not finished. It seems like they should be. As a baby, Alex was found in a trashcan, then brought to the Orphanage. Enough said. But then, much later, through meeting missionaries at those summer camps, Alex Krutov somehow came to the United States, became part of many families, graduated from college, began working. Horatio Alger. Another complete story about beating odds. Only Alex was not happy. He found himself, after a serious argument, wandering along a freeway in Southern California, thinking about Russia. And praying. He continued to hear about one childhood friend, then another, still in Russia, addicted, lost, in prison, or dead. So he went back. And with a lot of help, started the Harbor. And has tended to it ever since.

Alex smiles when he tells us he is forty, but his face is tight. Spending half a year in Russia and half a year traveling to raise money for support, the last few times we have met, Alex more and more talks about wanting his own family, wanting to be a father. He imagines all sorts of possibilities. As he does so, his "God works in mysterious ways" sounds less gloomy. He is currently working to start Harbors in other areas of Russia. Not too long ago, in Tolyatti (our Alex as well as the rest of us now knows where this is), through the support of a successful Muslim business woman in the community, Alex found himself inside a large warehouse-like building. He pictured for us, "A small coffee shop might go there; our mothers' program more toward the back; and we would still have room for teaching, maybe welding, maybe cooking, maybe computer classes. We'll see what happens."

We are looking forward to this seeing.

— XXII —

The Blessings We Need

A Sermon Given to First Presbyterian Church, Smithville

February 17, 2019

Thus says the Lord: Cursed are those who trust in mere mortals and make mere flesh their strength, whose hearts turn away from the Lord. They shall be like a shrub in the desert, and shall not see when relief comes. They shall live in the parched places of the wilderness, in an uninhabited salt land. Blessed are those who trust in the Lord, whose trust is the Lord. They shall be like a tree planted by water, sending out its roots by the stream. It shall not fear when heat comes, and its leaves shall stay green; in the year of drought it is not anxious, and it does not cease to bear fruit. The heart is devious above all else; it is perverse—who can understand it? I the Lord test the mind and search the heart, to give to all according to their ways, according to the fruit of their doings.

JEREMIAH 17:5–10 (NRSV)

Now if Christ is proclaimed as raised from the dead, how can some of you say there is no resurrection of the dead? If there is no resurrection of the dead, then Christ has not been raised; and if Christ has not been raised, then our proclamation has been in vain and your faith has been in vain. We are even found to be misrepresenting God, because we testified of God that he raised Christ—whom he did not raise if it is true that the dead are not raised. For if the dead are not raised, then Christ has not been raised. If Christ has not been raised, your faith is futile and you are still in your sins. Then those also who have died in Christ have perished. If for this life only we have hoped in Christ, we are of all people most to be pitied. But in fact Christ has been raised from the dead, the first fruits of those who have died.

I CORINTHIANS 15:12–20 (NRSV)

He came down with them and stood on a level place, with a great crowd of his disciples and a great multitude of people from all Judea, Jerusalem, and the coast of Tyre and Sidon. They had come to hear him and to be healed of their diseases; and those who were troubled with unclean spirits were cured. And all in the crowd were trying to touch him, for power came out from him and healed all of them. Then he looked up at his disciples and said: "Blessed are you who are poor, for yours is the kingdom of God. Blessed are you who are hungry now, for you will be filled. Blessed are you who weep now, for you will laugh. Blessed are you when people hate you, and when they exclude you, revile you, and defame you on account of the Son of Man. Rejoice in that day and leap for joy, for surely your reward is great in heaven; for that is what their ancestors did to the prophets. But woe to you who are rich, for you have received your consolation. Woe to you who are full now, for you will be hungry. Woe to you who are laughing now, for you will mourn and weep. Woe to you when all speak well of you, for that is what their ancestors did to the false prophets."

LUKE 6:17–26 (NRSV)

The Blessings We Need

WHEN I SAT DOWN with today's reading from 1 Corinthians, the last time I lived with these verses flooded back to me. I was visiting with my friend, Boyce, a sweet, sweet, effervescent, raconteur (he would have loved being called this) who served in the Army in Japan during and after the World War II. His time in that culture changed his life, and he loved to share story after story about the wonderful people he met as well as about what he saw, both the unimaginable devastation and the quiet, elegant culture that tried to hold its head up in the face of horror and loss. He also enjoyed very much talking about Henry and Alex which made me appreciate him all the more. He had a beautiful singing voice and would use it on occasion during conversation. It was so much fun to be with him. So of course, I was glad to be able to visit him when he was in the hospital.

Boyce had a not altogether explainable cluster of symptoms that he was working through: weakness, dizziness, a little pain, some heart irregularities. We talked about things coming up in the church, about his ranch, and his family. But over the next several weeks, in and out of the hospital, in and out of rehab, his symptoms got consistently worse. One evening, Boyce told me that he had cancer. I wasn't expecting this. Nor was Boyce. He spoke of his hopes for recovery. We sat quietly for a while. Then Boyce took my hand and said, "I know I am an old man, so this sounds funny. But I have so much to give. I am not ready to die.

I've been going to church all my life, but I don't know now what I think about any of it."

I was still processing the information that Boyce had cancer. Because it didn't seem to me that he should have, because it didn't seem possible that this man who was so full of life was about to face fighting that horrible disease. So I took in what he said slowly, a little after he said it. And as I was making my way through each of Boyce's words, Paul's words (generally, I'm not that great about remembering scripture) came alongside Boyce's so that I knew I had to speak them. I told Boyce that if Jesus were not raised, our hopes, our faith, so much of our lives would be empty; that we would be foolish, pitiable people. Boyce smiled at me and asked, "Do you think so?" "Yes. And this is the center of our faith, of what you and I believe," I said. After that, we spent a good bit of time talking about the ways in which each of us had experienced God's love in our lives. And we prayed for Boyce's future. For you see, Boyce had a future. He is no longer here with us, but he still has. Knowing Boyce, if he were able, he would be delighted to tell you more than you wanted to know about that future right now.

The same kind of disconnect, of looking at something in the only way you know how but then being told that what you should make of it is not at all what you would normally think, makes me pause whenever I come to Jesus's beatitudes. Christ died. But Christ is risen. Boyce died. But Boyce is alive. And then there are today's poor and hungry and weeping, the ones who are hated, excluded, called evil because of their faith. We are told they are "blessed"; the Greek can also be translated, "happy." Are they? They must be because Jesus says so. But how exactly does this work? What is Jesus saying, and what is he calling us to do? How are we supposed to look at our world?

I usually find when things don't make sense, it's a good idea to back up to the last moment when they did. Maybe it is easier to start with Jesus's "woes." "Woe to you who are rich," "for you have received your consolation or comfort or coming alongside." As we listen for all we are able to hear, we might look around with the rich (who most likely we recognize as being at least very close

The Blessings We Need

kin) and say to ourselves, "Will all my stuff do in a time of crisis? Will what I have piled up get me through grief and illness and change and loss? Do I have comfort enough? I am full now and am laughing, but what will happen when I start to be hungry again. What will happen when next I must mourn or weep?" As I ask such questions, I start to understand Jesus's "woes." Because, in fact, the consolations I have stored won't do. Woe to me. So much of what I have so carefully planned, if I am truthful about it, is not really able to hold me up, will not get me through.

Before Jesus starts talking, Luke tells us that "he came down and stood on a level place with a great crowd of his disciples and a great multitude of people from all Judea, Jerusalem, and the coast of Tyre and Sidon. They had come to hear him and to be healed of their diseases; and those who were troubled with unclean spirits were cured. And all in the crowd were trying to touch him, for the power came out from him and healed all of them." Maybe as we are trying to make sense of Jesus's happy poor, hungry, and weeping, we should pay closer attention to what is going on around Jesus as he begins his blessings and woes. Because then and there, at the moment Jesus is speaking, the playing field is leveled. The poor, hungry, and weeping are being taken care of. The picture Luke gives us suggests that all that sweaty, sick, worried, hungry, diseased multitude matters so much to God that God chooses to come alongside and show God's love, case by case, person by person, sad heart by sad heart. Jesus acts before we hear him speak. And his actions demonstrate the very blessings that we have such a hard time understanding.

As we return to "blessed are the poor, for yours is the kingdom of God," let us really hear Jesus's "yours." Who is Jesus's "you?" Whose do we think the kingdom of God is? Off the top of our heads, perhaps our "you" would be a person who is not poor, who has worked hard and so far has avoided catastrophe and has a winning smile? Or maybe a successful politician or the person from that nice family? Does the kingdom belong to those who can win it or take it or are in the right place at the right time? What sort of kingdom would that be?

Jeremiah tells us that when we trust in mere mortals and make mere flesh our strength, we are like shrubs in the desert, and we will not see when relief comes. So often, until it is almost too late, we don't even seem to know we need relief. We get comfortable enough with our ever-shrinking pieces of family and home and whatever else it is we hold onto. We are certain that we are doing what we ought and that we don't need anything else. And somehow, we come to believe that this is what blessing amounts to.

"Living in the parched places of the wilderness, in an uninhabited salt land." How did we settle in here? Jeremiah tells us the condition of our hearts places us. Our trust in the wrong place assures that we will remain in the wrong place. So that Jesus comes among us and says, "Don't worry." And "blessed are you when you are poor." And "yours is the kingdom of God." And we say, "We are all very well here, thank you. Why don't you go on down the road?" "If Christ is proclaimed as raised from the dead, how can some of you say there is no resurrection of the dead?" I'll tell you how. We sink down into wanting only what we can imagine.

Because we know best. Right? Of course, not. Jesus says "yours," I think, in part to chase us out of the desert. Surely, when we hear Jesus say "you," we at first hear him talking to us and connect with the people Jesus signals out, "You who are poor, you who are hungry, you who are weeping." We hear and know that God is for the weak; the ones who lose, the ones we too often ignore. But we might go farther: we might go ahead and admit it: everyone one of us may be, might be, will be poor, mourning, weeping. And as we stand by and watch person after person come to Jesus and be healed, we might say to ourselves, "Oh my Lord, I want what you are giving. It's not so good standing alone by myself. Receiving your care is coming into the kingdom of heaven. Sharing that care is doing your will."

Should we walk up to Jesus with that ragged crowd? "Oh dear Lord, I want your blessing. For myself. For all those struggling around me. For the sake of your kingdom. You have opened my heart. Fill it with your love." What else might we say to Jesus, if we were standing on that level field, if we placed ourselves

The Blessings We Need

alongside Jesus's poor, struggling "you"? Jesus offers us a blessing. Will we take it up?

— XXIII —

The Hole In The Middle

A ROUGH TRANSLATION OF Acts 8:26–39: *And an angel of the Lord spoke to Philip, saying "Arise and go south upon the way going down from Jerusalem into Gaza." (This is a wilderness.) And having arisen, he went and, look, an Ethiopian man, a eunuch, a man of power, of Candice, the Queen of Ethiopians, who was over all her treasure, a man who had come into Jerusalem to bow down and worship. And he was returning and sitting on his chariot and he was reading the prophet Isaiah. And the spirit said to Philip, "Go to (him) and join/ glue yourself to this chariot." And having run up, Philip heard him reading Isaiah the prophet, and he said, "Hey, do you indeed know the things you are reading?" And he said, "For how am I able unless someone will guide me?" And he urged Philip, having come up, to sit with him. And the passage of scripture which he was reading was this one: "as a sheep to slaughter, he was led, and as a lamb facing the one sheering is speechless, so he does not open his mouth. In his humiliation, his choice was taken away. Who can tell of his family for his life was taken from the earth?" The eunuch, having answered Philip, he said, "I beseech you, concerning whom does the prophet say this thing? Concerning himself or another?" And having opened his mouth and having begun from the scripture, he preached Jesus to him. And as they were going according to the way, they came to some water and the eunuch says, "Look, water. What forbids me to be baptized?"* [some manuscripts add: *And Philip said to him, "If you believe with the whole of your heart, it is lawful," And having*

The Hole In The Middle

answered, he said, "I believe the son of God to be Jesus Christ."] and he ordered the chariot to stop and they both went down into the water, Philip and the eunuch, and he baptized him. And when they went up out of the water, a spirit of the Lord seized Philip, and the eunuch did not see him any longer, but went his way rejoicing.

— XXIV —

Philip and the Eunuch

WHAT IS THE KINGDOM of God like when Jesus leaves? Perhaps Jesus gives us a glimpse at the end of Luke's gospel: "When [Jesus] had said this, he showed them his hands and feet. And while they, because of joy and amazement, still did not believe it, he asked them, "Do you have anything here to eat?" (24:40–41) Here, we know Jesus because we know his parts are real. Maybe when the initial joy and amazement are over, especially after Jesus is gone from the scene, the disciples-turned-apostles returned to the hands, the feet, the fact that Jesus could eat; maybe these facts held up as they tried to explain what exactly the resurrection was and did. They must have held up enough for us to have them. Yet, if the resurrection in Luke's gospel honors the solidness of this kind of knowing, the limitations of parts representing wholes show themselves almost immediately as we think about the people who wander about our own landscapes. We celebrate when we see feet, hands, eating connected to the Lord we love, when we are able to move from part to a whole. But when we only have the parts, we are unsure. We want to know and to be known better.

The curious story in Acts chapter 8 where Philip meets an Ethiopian eunuch centers on the problem of parts serving as shorthand for wholes. Unlike so many others who meet apostles in Acts, the eunuch is never named. All we know is that this "Ethiopian" does not belong to himself. He is a man of Candice, the Queen of the Ethiopians, "a man of power . . . over all her treasure" (8:27),

Philip and the Eunuch

but he is also a nation-state slave. And being this sort of slave, he is, almost by definition, less than whole. Worse, as we meet him, being a eunuch is this man's identity; one part of him has become who he is.

Of course, such a reduction has consequences. At this time, it was customary for eunuch-slaves from northern Africa to be castrated and also to some degree to be dismembered. Besides the personal grief and misery inherent in such a condition, being a eunuch in the world of Acts has peculiar religious implications. For example, no matter how much a eunuch might admire Jewish teachings and tradition, he could not be circumcised. Regardless of his political importance, the eunuch in Luke's story most likely would not be allowed to enter much of the temple. Because we know the eunuch has traveled a great distance to worship in Jerusalem (8:27) and because we are introduced to him reading Isaiah aloud as he travels, struggling with Scripture, we feel we are in the presence of someone longing to understand God and, at least partially, blocked in his ability to do so. What is blocking him is the part he has become. The irony, or more nearly, tragedy that this condition results from his not being whole, from his missing a part, deserves to be noticed both to underscore the sterile harshness resulting from so many of the laws that, by this time, had grown up around circumcision (an issue that will resurface soon and more than once in Acts) and the terrible cost that part-without-getting-to-the-whole identity exacts. We know the eunuch is looking for God and that he is not finding him.

And then the Holy Spirit brings Philip to the eunuch. In climbing up into the eunuch's chariot, Philip presents the Christian response to legalistic shunning. Here, in the wilderness, a Jew and a eunuch can together trouble themselves over Scripture, not over each other; they do so, they come together, at the express direction of the Holy Spirit. Luke centers their experience upon the eunuch's reading Isaiah 53:7–8, verses Luke repeats in full. From the point of view of the eunuch, these verses may seem painfully familiar:

> As a sheep to slaughter, he was led, and as a lamb facing
> the one sheering is speechless, so he does not open his

mouth. In his humiliation, his choice was taken away. Who can tell of his family for his life was taken from the earth?

Whatever we are to think about the connection between Isaiah and Jesus, in the presence of the eunuch, we read these verses in a way we have not read them before, with our heads down. What more terrible picture of forced castration could the eunuch find in Scripture? Or what picture of forced castration, from the point of view of the one castrated, could the eunuch find anywhere else in Scripture? Reading with the eunuch, reading the eunuch into the passage, we understand his own suffering and loss, the suffering and loss inherent in his forced, part-without-the-whole identity. And we understand why he is stuck. When he asks, "Concerning whom does the prophet say this thing?" (v. 34), the eunuch wants to know who connects to him, who might understand his problem and pain.

We are told that Philip "preached Jesus to him" (v. 35). Isaiah serves as a bridge where Jesus and the eunuch meet. If the eunuch knows that Jesus has suffered like he has, the eunuch may find himself to be included with Jesus. His response suggests that this happens for him. When a few manuscripts add v. 37 to suggest that the eunuch's baptism is somehow contingent upon his statement of belief, they miss what has happened to the eunuch. As we meet him, the eunuch has always hoped to believe. But he needs to be healed. Like all the lame, blind, sick people throughout the New Testament whose circumstances have reduced to one painful part of who they are. Verse 27's "Look" ("an Ethiopian man, a eunuch") beginning Philip's encounter with the eunuch repeats in v. 36, "Look" ("water"). "Water" is counterpoised with "eunuch." Given the joy with which the eunuch closes his story, we can assume baptism does for him what he needs: it serves as a sign that he is clean, reborn, part but connected to a whole; he has received salvation. Because Christ is contiguous to him, the eunuch is able to find him.

— XXV —

The Floor Drops Out

For about two months during the summer between seventh and eight grade, I moved with my family to Norfolk, Virginia. It was supposed to be a permanent move, and my guess is that my Dad thought it could not come soon enough. About six months before we left, I went over to our neighbors and asked them if they wanted me to walk their dog. Scot and Lynda were both teachers; they didn't have children, and they were always very kind to me. Scot introduced me to checkers and regularly invited me over to play board games. He ran a summer youth program at his church and brought me with him. I loved Winnie, their dog, almost as much as I loved Lui, my dog. Practically every weekend and most summer mornings, Lui, Winnie, and I covered the neighborhood. This particular day, Lynda came to the door and told me that I probably better not come over anymore. I didn't understand and went home. My mother became hysterical, and my father was silent. Years later, my father told me Lynda and Scot believed, with good reason, that my mother had stolen their silver. We needed to move.[1]

When we got to Norfolk, my parents hardly spoke to one another. We lived on base. Before we had left, my father told me we

---

1. While I do not know if she would agree with the diagnosis, I have come to accept that my mother suffers from bipolar disorder. Of course, I did not understand this as a child (or as an adult for many years). What might have been for her, for us, if she had received appropriate treatment?

could not bring Lui because the base didn't allow dogs. We gave Lui to another family. When we got there, everyone around us had a dog. We spent one day driving to Williamsburg, mostly in silence. We arrived, and my father discovered that it was going to cost, I can't remember how much, something like sixty or seventy dollars, maybe more, for the five of us to walk around the tourist part of the city and see the sights. We got back in the car and drove home. A tropical depression hit Norfolk. Someone had left a window open in our Travel-All which was the most wonderful car we ever had. After three days of solid rain, flooding, and our staying inside, my father went out and saw water up to and over the seats. He got the water out, but mold overcame the car. Not able to bear being in Norfolk, I told my mother how much I missed Lui. She said that she loved a man named Ed in San Antonio, and that she was taking Eric, Jason, and me on the plane early in the morning, and that I wasn't to say anything, and that we would get Lui back. I lay awake all night. I didn't know what to do. My mother left a note for my father. I never saw the Travel-All again. I will never forget the note sitting on our kitchen table. All my life since, I have not been able to escape my Dad reading that note.

Back in San Antonio, we lived with my mother and Ed in a small apartment. We didn't get Lui. Ed sold fire alarms (later, beyond his time with us, he went to the penitentiary because he set fire to a house in order to scare people into buying alarm systems). Eric cried all the time. Jason talked so fast that only Eric could understand him. Our mother was irritable, ready to fight, insisting that we take her side against the neighbors, against the store where she worked, against whomever. She was mad at our father; mad at Ed; mad at her work; mad at us. She drank wine late into every night. I wanted to love her. Once I went with her to a department store; we looked at clothes together for a while, then I watched as she covered some lipstick with her hand, and it ended in her purse. I almost threw up. Ed and mom often would light candles at night when they drank. Ed would put his finger back and forth through the flames. I read to my brothers in the bedroom, but after they were asleep, if I showed myself, my mother would want to

The Floor Drops Out

fight. She often ended by threatening to send me away somewhere. Somehow, I couldn't imagine anything worse. One afternoon, she began to scream and scream at me, and I ran out of the house to get away from her. Outside, I did not know how I would go back in. I found myself walking to the highway near our apartments. And I thought if I ran across it and got hit by a car, it might be for the best. So I did. But I didn't get hit by a car. I ended up in a disemboweled field where construction was about to begin. I lay down in the dirt and felt myself shaking because I was crying so hard. I didn't see how I could keep on living. As I cried myself out, I prayed to something to come and take me. I don't know how long I lay there, but after a while I kept my eyes closed and felt something warm filling me up; I felt light and not scared anymore. I was somehow not alone.

— XXVI —

Piecing Things Together

IN ACTS, FAITH COMES through the laying on of hands, through being blinded, through healing, through hearing, here and there through the unexpected, even unimaginable intervention of the Holy Spirit. Substituting "Holy Spirit" for "faith" indicates the strength of their connection, for in Acts, the Holy Spirit comes through the laying on of hands, healing, hearing, and however else the Holy Spirit wants to come. Sometimes faith is believing; sometimes we find in Acts people who have at least a kind of faith and, because of this, they learn to believe. Acts unsettles "correct" belief as it works out the tensions between Judaism and the emerging church. Most important, in Acts, answers, definitions, understandings depend upon where we start reading, whose stories we meet. So as we read through the many speeches of Acts, we are given multiple histories of salvation, the story of the Jews, the story of Jesus's death, the story of the general revelation of God in the world, the story of Paul, even that story revisited. At the same time that we see Christianity working out the individual salvations of eunuchs, prison guards, tanners, crippled beggars, Roman officials, a Pharisee, we see Christianity undermining the Jewish assertion that its whole is complete as well as the Roman assertion that its whole is complete. To know God or to know Jesus or the Holy Spirit through a name (for example, 10:15) or a voice (9:4) or light (26:13) or the sound of wind (2:2) is to know something certain and partial.

Piecing Things Together

This kind of knowledge allows one to operate in a broken world. To walk forward step by step rather than take a metaphoric leap. When God is in a name or a voice or a light or the sound of the wind, we have to give up our systems and pay close attention to what is right in front of us. We have to start with the particulars and see what they are connected to. We find ourselves in something close to, but not exactly, experimental. I can't help thinking about Wittgenstein again because he makes, for me, such a useful distinction:

> 6.363 The process of induction is the process of assuming the simplest law that can be made to harmonize with our existence.
>
> 6.3631 This process, however, has no logical foundation (no part of deep structure) but only a psychological one. It is clear that there are no grounds for believing that the simplest course of events will really happen.[1]

If we substitute for Wittgenstein's "deep structure," Luke's "the kingdom of God/heaven," we might see that the "simplest laws" we make to get back inside Jesus's metaphors, the kingdom we imagine and are pretty sure of, may have all sorts of psychological value for us but may not hold up. It turns out we are not, as our primary task, proving anything (maybe because we can't). Instead, we are going somewhere, and what is right in front of us is able to direct us, perhaps, if we press a little harder, to the next place, to the outskirts of kingdom we are looking for.

---

1. Wittgenstein, *Tractatus Logico-Philosophicus*, 179–80.

— XXVII —

Turning Around

Mr. Przgoda taught Saturday school at Temple Bethel, my family's temple, off and on while I was in sixth grade. His father died in the Holocaust. One day, we had all made it to class, even the very late stragglers, but Mr. Przgoda was missing. Someone claimed that there was a ten minute waiting rule. Time passed. We felt certain that there must be a fifteen minute rule (no one had the chuzpa to go ahead and leave after ten minutes). Two paper footballs appeared and flew across our tables, then a shrill voice hushed us, insisting that we be quiet so that the rest of the school would not know that we had no teacher. Suddenly, the door banged open. Mr. Przgoda burst into the room, scattering paper, throwing chairs, and yelling what sounded like slurs or military words. I don't know exactly how long this went on. Then he stopped (I think he saw how frightened we were). And he said, "This is what it was like. To be a Jew in Germany. Only after they broke into your house, they took you away."

At that moment, I collapsed, maybe for the first time, into what? Grief and guilt and anxiety and terrible anger. Mr. Przgoda's father, is this what happened to him? How could you be innocent and have your world turned upside down? And how do you help people who are already dead? Mr. Przgoda wanted us to remember forever what had happened in Germany. The rest of my life so far, I have been working out this remembering. The probability of unbearable disaster, of unrelenting hate, has informed and infected so much of how I understand history, humanity, God. What is post-modern education, if it is not grappling with terror; reading, talking about, writing about, re-considering that war and all the countless genocides, petty sadisms, racisms, tyrannies, oppressions, injustice, hatred, and misery that make up history, that define the human heart? But what to do? How do you stop madness?

Mr. Przgoda, whom I loved dearly, insisted that we start by not running away from facts. He was a very brave person. He wanted us to face things. Part of our Saturday School experience was to learn about other religions, to compare Judaism to them. When we got to Christianity, Mr. Przgoda explained that Christians believed Jesus was killed because he wanted to change what was wrong in the world, but then he rose from the dead. I was a little stunned. "Do you mean like in a story?" "No. They believe Jesus died and then was no longer dead." Some of my classmates began to talk about zombies. I couldn't figure out what Jesus's being alive, then dead, then alive, (where was he now) had to do with anything. "Why do they say that?" I wanted to find out what the point of all this was. Mr. Przgoda misunderstood. "Because some of them saw him alive after he was dead." "Who? As a ghost?" "No. Christians say maybe a hundred people saw him, and he wasn't a ghost." I thought about a hundred people. My friends were getting tired of my keeping this going, but I had to ask, "What do we say?" Mr. Przgoda told us that the people who saw Jesus after he was dead had loved Jesus very much because Jesus was a great man. They were so upset by his death that they saw what they needed, what they wanted. Didn't we sometimes just see what we wanted to see?

A mass hallucination. I suppose that made sense to me. I felt like it needed to because I wanted to have the right answer. Being smart, knowing the right answer, is like a power ring. All that focus, a question, an answer, a concept to master, means not being distracted by the disruption surrounding you. It means you are getting somewhere. And I wanted to get somewhere. Each Saturday morning, my class spent some time learning Hebrew phonetically so that we could read or seem like we were reading for our bar and bat mitzvahs. We were all a little behind, and Mr. Przgoda was given the task of catching us up. When it became difficult, then impossible because of the stress of our family's splitting up, for me to continue with the class, I missed Mr. Przgoda. At my cousin's bar mitzvah two years later, after I was no longer going to Saturday school, I listened to my cousin reading in Hebrew a passage from the Old Testament about ephahs of grain and numbers of sheep. Mr. Pryzgoda would have helped me find a better passage. In our class, we may not have gotten very far with Hebrew, but we had been closing in on God.

As I got a little older, I didn't think much about Mr. Pryzgoda, probably for the same reason that I cannot go into the Holocaust Museum. I understand that I should; I just can't. I wanted to be a Jew though. The party following my cousin's bar mitzvah lasted deep into the morning. My uncle and aunt had us bunny-hopping down the stairs from the attic to the basement; 50s, 60s, and 70s music from a stereo, from adults singing at the tops of their voices, from random drumming and clapping; platters of sliced meats and cheeses, twisted breads and bagels, pastries, cake, chocolates; and all the conversation, the politics, the jokes, laughter; how could you not want all that? Ephahs, sheep, Hebrew did not matter. These were and are my people. Because they took me in. And because we have so much fun.

In high school, Mimi Hendricks was my connection to Judaism. We were smart girls in the smart classes. She had dreamy eyes, one a little blue, one a little green. And she was very much part of the Jewish world all that was perpetually going on at my home kept me just outside. She sat near me in French; we made fun of Mademoiselle Roche who wore so much mascara that you could count the clumps of her eyelashes back at our desks, who had been a cheerleader at our school years before, and who on mum days covered herself with so many mums she jingled as she walked. After class one day, Mimi announced that it was her birthday. Somehow, I thought I should have known this. So I sort of claimed to have known this and wished her happy birthday. She caught me in my lie. "You didn't remember, did you?" My hands got sweaty. "Of course, I did. But I left your present at home." (What did I just

Turning Around

say?) "You didn't get me anything." "Of course, I did. I'll bring it tomorrow." "What is it?" "A surprise."

A surprise to me. I had no money. I mean no money. We ate a lot of canned beans and hot dogs at our house; I was on the free lunch program at school, but I didn't eat lunch very often because I was embarrassed. My mother drove a fancy car. I didn't think I ought to be getting free lunches. When I got home, I went out into the garage behind our duplex where my mother kept knick-knacks she sold to her design clients. In a box of small clay figures from Guatemala, there was a curved painted man, resting on his chest; one of his legs in the air opened up so that it became a bud vase. I thought it was wonderful. I wrapped it up and gave it to Mimi the next day.

When Mimi opened it, she smiled at me the way we smiled at Mme. Roche. "This is exactly the sort of thing *you* might give someone." I wasn't quite sure what she meant, but I could see she didn't think much of the vase. I looked at his painted face and wondered what I had done. That night, my mother seemed like she was in a stable place. I told her about the gift. I should not have. Around our house, we had gotten to the point that we mostly did not answer the phone, or, if one of my brothers were around, my mother would hand the phone to him and let him confuse the credit card police on the line. A glass of wine in her hand, my mother started normally enough, but ended up nowhere anyone wanted to be. She had been drinking earlier. She ran out into the garage and looked at her boxes. Then she came in and started screaming. I don't know for how long. She just kept repeating that I had to get that statue back, that I had stolen it, that she had plans for it.

The funny thing is that she was sort of right. Disgusted, I watched her face and mouth moving up and down, watched her brutal crying and yelling, maybe about the statue. But I also knew that, in a way, I had sold out Eric, Jason, Mom. I supposed (I did understand that this wasn't much) we could have used whatever money the jumping man might bring. And then Mimi invited me to spend the night, something that had never happened between us before. Maybe because of the gift? When she dropped me off, my mother insisted that I come out in the morning with the vase. I went into a bright, bright, giant house, filled with all sorts of very tasty and healthy snacks, and beige furniture. We played games with Mimi's parents. Her father called Mimi, "Princess." Under some pretense, I went up to Mimi's bedroom, where my stuff was, and started looking for the statue. It was on a top shelf in her closet. Everyone was calling me from downstairs. I yelled something about my shoes (which made no sense), then climbed on a chair, rescued the little man, and put him at the bottom of my bag, under everything else I had. I went back downstairs, overly exuberant. My head was light. I could tell Mimi's parents thought I was boorish, but I kept talking and laughing. I knew during the night Mimi would notice the statue was missing from her closet.

But she didn't. I also never was invited back. I wanted nothing to do with my mother's pouting when I handed her the statue. She was no martyr. The drama of it all amounted to squat. All of it. It could all go to hell. It is hard to see things clearly, but it is also freeing, or so I thought. Mme. Roche was ridiculous. Mimi could not be my friend. My history teacher, my chemistry teacher, they were both idiots. The anguish, the pimples, the hashing and rehashing of school relationships, the rules, sitting and listening to people talk and talk and talk, I could barely stand it. And then there was my mother. Would I be bound to her craziness forever? What would happen to her? How would my brothers stay safe with my father so far away?

With the help of theater classes, I floated through weeks and weeks. Being in plays, reading poetry out loud, working on scenes for competitions, I accumulated friends, most of whom were floating along with me, absorbed, like me, in their own struggles. Concentrating on whatever project we had, I found myself calm, living deep down inside someone else by saying certain words. Whispering lines in the library with Randy, I would interrupt to explain what I thought what we were saying meant. I must have been insufferable, but it all seemed so important: to get it right, to figure someone else out. Randy invited me to go to church with him. When I found out that he was a Southern Baptist, I couldn't

Turning Around

believe it. Because I was pretty sure among all the Christians, these were the stupidest. He kept bugging me. And I liked him. Our scene was going well. So I finally went with him.

Trinity Baptist Church, not too far from Temple Bethel, was light and cavernous and filled with men in suits (I was wearing jeans) and women with hair piled high, high above their heads. Everyone seemed to know exactly what to do. Sing. Sing some more. Listen. Put money in a dish. And sing again. I fumbled through the service. Automatic worship. I had seen it before. I had read words, read words in phonetic Hebrew even, at the right times. For what? But I went with Randy again. As I sat in the pew, I thought about my father and was angry with myself for going along with this. Randy wasn't worth it. People around me talked Texan; they seemed like they couldn't think themselves out of a paper bag. I went a third time. During the service, I decided I would not come back. I don't remember what the pastor was talking about, but as he spoke, I tore apart everyone I saw, everyone I could think of. He was stupid. She was stupid. That one would never see how stupid he was. My heart moved so quickly that I lost my breath. It hurt, hurt like the worst headache, to be so alone. Better than everyone else, better than all these people I didn't need.

What did I need? Nothing. No one. I found myself crying. I tried to focus on not crying. Scratching a scab on my arm, I accidentally ripped it open. What had I done? I was still crying as quietly as I could. All sorts of things came to me, nonsense, lying, bitterness, meanness, the Holocaust and that little statue, it was all there. I could not get out of it. The pastor was proclaiming something about the love of God in Jesus. My sleeve was soaked, a little with blood, but mostly with my crying. I was hardly aware of Randy sitting next to me. It was hopeless. I was hopeless. I looked up in time to see and then hear the pastor say the word, "help." And somehow, in that split second of looking up, in the movement of my chin or in the music I was hearing around me that I had not noticed, I felt the possibility of possibility. Something bigger than me. Someone inviting me to back off the ledge. And come inside.

— XXVIII —

A God Who Lifts Up

*A Sermon Given to
First Presbyterian Church, Smithville*

December 2, 2018

*"The days are coming," declares the Lord, "when I will
fulfill the good promise I made to the people of Israel
and Judah. In those days and at that time I will make
a righteous Branch sprout from David's line; he will do
what is just and right in the land. In those days Judah
will be saved and Jerusalem will live in safety. This is
the name by which it will be called:
The Lord Our Righteous Savior."*

JEREMIAH 33:14–16 (NIV)

*How can we thank God enough for you in return for all
the joy we have in the presence of our God because of
you? Night and day we pray most earnestly that we may
see you again and supply what is lacking in your faith.
Now may our God and Father himself and our Lord
Jesus clear the way for us to come to you. May the Lord*

A God Who Lifts Up

make your love increase and overflow for each other and for everyone else, just as ours does for you. May he strengthen your hearts so that you will be blameless and holy in the presence of our God and Father when our Lord Jesus comes with all his holy ones.

I THESSALONIANS 3:9–13 (NIV)

And Mary said, "My soul magnifies the Lord, and my spirit rejoices in God my Savior, for he has looked with favor on the lowliness of his servant. Surely, from now on all generations will call me blessed; for the Mighty One has done great things for me, and holy is his name. His mercy is for those who fear him from generation to generation. He has shown strength with his arm; he has scattered the proud in the thoughts of their hearts. He has brought down the powerful from their thrones, and lifted up the lowly; he has filled the hungry with good things, and sent the rich away empty. He has helped his servant Israel, in remembrance of his mercy, according to the promise he made to our ancestors, to Abraham and to his descendants forever."

LUKE 1:46–55 (NRSV)

A God Who Lifts Up

LISTENING TO THE RADIO a couple of months ago, I was held by a news story about migrant people banding together, walking into Mexico and toward our border. At that time, there were around three thousand people in a small town in Guatemala, waiting to cross over into Mexico. The story began with background: President Trump's voice and tweets promising to send extra troops, even to close our borders if necessary, followed by some analysis of the practicality of this, came before descriptions of the border between Guatemala and Mexico where the migrants were and the town square and other places they were sleeping. Turning to the scene at hand, the reporter interviewed some of the very poor people in that tiny Guatemalan town who were passing out food and medical supplies as they were able. As I was tracing in my mind a map of Honduras, Guatemala, Belize, Mexico, then the United States, the reporter began to interview other people at the scene. An older local man said that he hoped the migrants would be alright. An aid worker described how hot it was. My thoughts wandered from all that I was hearing to the politics, fear, to all the problems surrounding this group as a current issue.

Maybe my just mentioning these migrants has brought to your minds the very same politics and fear. Maybe you are thinking about your own positions on the subject or just wishing we could talk about something else. We will. But when I read Mary's prayer or song or proclamation, this week's gospel text, to get ready for this sermon, I suddenly found myself back listening to the radio. What happened next, as I pulled into the Lowe's parking lot, was that the interviewer started talking to a twelve-year-old boy. Quietly, the boy explained he was traveling with the migrants because at home gangs had killed his father, and his mother was very sick, and she told him he needed to get away. She was afraid for his life. He didn't want to go, but his mother was so afraid for him that he left. He said the walking was very, very hard. He was headed to the United States where people were good, where he would work and go to school and send money home to his mother. He said there must be justice in the world. Justice and safety, that is what he wanted.

Sitting in my car, I prayed for this boy, but I also felt helpless. I want so much for him what he wants. Don't you? Don't you want for him, for you, for us, justice and safety? And a place where we are not afraid; where we can count on people; they can count on us; where we can work and go to school and take care of our families? "In those days and at that time I will make a righteous Branch sprout from David's line; he will do what is just and right in the land. In those days Judah will be saved and Jerusalem will live in safety. And this is the name it will be called: The Lord is our righteousness." That boy, away from his family, walking and walking, no doubt tired and frightened, is hoping for Jeremiah's vision. Oh, that we could give this vision to him, that we could bring him right now to a place of safety and justice. And his family.

But how to do it? I mean this as an open question. How shall we do it? Jeremiah tells us the Lord will make a righteous Branch; the Lord will provide the Righteous Savior we need. So do we hunker down and wait? Watch the misery all around us and say something like, "Some day this will all be over"? You know, Christians have thought like this in the past, and maybe some do today. But why long for justice and safety and righteousness, why be so discouraged when someone does something wrong, why care at all, if there is nothing we might or can do? Does God give us our sense of right and wrong just to mess with us? To make us feel bad?

Surely not. We look for a coming day when a righteous branch will do what is just and right in the land. Looking for that day, we move toward it. As we do, a crazy thing happens, what theologians might call the mystery of Advent. We find that the coming day we hope for is also here. God is coming, and God is here. So that we don't put our light under a bushel or ignore the lavish invitation we receive to come to a party (I hope you remember these parables). Instead, we act. We get ready. We thank God for the sense of justice and mercy he has given us, and we ask him what he wants us to do with what we know. And we expect that God will answer.

Even though we might not expect what God's answer will be. Think about Mary, not too much older than the boy I heard on the radio. It is not that God will do this, that, or the other. Mary's soul glorifies the Lord because "the Mighty One has done great things." "He has performed mighty deeds with his arm; he has scattered those who are proud in their inmost thoughts. He has brought down rulers from their thrones but has lifted up the humble. He has filled the hungry with good things but has sent the rich away empty." God does what we cannot imagine: our God works salvation for us and for all creation. God has done and is doing and will do this.

Our beautiful passage marks the moment when suddenly Mary finds out how. Mary herself turns out to be part of God's work. A teenage girl from a poor, subjugated race in one of what seems like the most God-forsaken outpost of the Roman empire trusts God her Savior and steps out because of this trust and becomes Mary with an illuminated capital "M," the mother of our Lord, the one who knows God is for us, no matter how low our circumstance. We trust God. And God answers. "I have saved. I save. I will save. I am the justice and safety and love and righteousness you long for. I am coming, and I am here." And Mary and you and me, along with that dear, dear boy; we are all invited in.

Once we begin to trust this, one we make our first move, our world often becomes topsy turvy. Things we believed so important turn out not to be. The process of sorting all this out, of continuing to move toward God on trust, can be, at times, the hardest walk we have ever taken. I don't know what will happen next to the boy I heard on the radio. I'm praying for him, and I hope you will too. I also pray that his voice will be in my mind when I have before me something that I might do now. Surely, when she saw her son die on that cross, Mary was completely broken. It seemed so much like the proud had won. But we know what happened.

And we know what happens now. The horrible yes, the disasters and injustice and misery and loss. But also the baby who is about to born into the world. The hope that has been and is and is coming. As that hope works its way through our lives and through our world, we find we have the strength to do the next thing. Strange as it may seem, we begin to be able to love the people around us, maybe in ways we haven't been able to before. Things aren't quite what we thought. And even our smallest faith, hope, and love break open the possibility that things can be not what we had imagined, but what they should be.

We have a picture. We have so many pictures. Paul comes to people he has never met, people in the worst sort of personal and political messes, shares his faith, hope, and love, and today, we are still caught up in what happened next. Paul's letters describe the transforming of a world. People who had no reason to care for one

A God Who Lifts Up

another; indeed, may have had good reason not to care, through sharing in that faith, hope and love, change how they see. So what they see changes. So that suddenly they find they earnestly love one another and want the best for each other and their community.

So that Paul thinks about them, writes to them, hopes to be with them, the rest of his travels. His wish for them extends to us: "May the Lord make your love increase and overflow for each other and everyone else. . . . May he strengthen your hearts so that you will be blameless and holy in the presence of our God and Father when our Lord Jesus comes with all his holy ones." The Lord is here and is coming. Let our hearts be strengthened so that we might love like we never have before and do the good work that is before us to do.

Amen.

— XXIX —

What Does This Thing Wish To Be?

How might I translate something I cannot imagine? Here's my latest attempt at Acts 2:1–12: *And in the to be fulfilled day of Pentecost, they were all together at the same place. And a sound came suddenly out of heaven just as a violent wind blowing, and it filled the whole house where they were sitting. And being divided tongues like fire were seen by them, and they sat on each one of them. And all were filled of a holy spirit and began to speak with other languages just as the spirit gave them to speak. And there were in Jerusalem, Jews living, devout men from all nations under heaven. And this sound having happened, the crowd came together, and they were confused because they were hearing them speaking unto each one in his own dialect. And they were amazed, and they were marveling saying, "Look, are not all these men, the ones speaking, Galileans? And how are we ourselves hearing us, each one in his own dialect in which we were born? Parthians and Medes and Elamites and the ones living in Mesopotamia, Judea, and Cappadocia, Pontus and Asia, Phyrgia and Pamphylia, Egypt and the parts of Libya near Cyrene, and the visiting Romans, Jews and proselytes, Cretans and Arabs, we hear them speaking in our own tongues the great things of God." And they were all amazed/stood outside of themselves and were greatly perplexed, another to another saying, "What does this thing wish to be?"/"What does this thing mean?"*

— XXX —

What Acts Acts Out

ACTS IS NOT so much about community or the beginnings of a community. It is about, well, acts. About making a move through the Holy Spirit and seeing what comes next. Luke gives us a slowly developing picture of the here and coming kingdom of God. We travel to this kingdom by peculiar and roundabout ways. We think we are building a church; we are part of a body. We are "all together at the same place" (2:1). But we are also living in a "deep structure" of which we may not be aware; we are living in a "to be fulfilled day" (2:1). And the question becomes, "How will we see this? How will we know where we are?"

The story of the Holy Spirit's appearance at Pentecost beginning chapter 2 kick-starts what becomes Christianity by pointing us away from our own imaginings. After the crucifixion, some of Jesus's followers, heart-broken men and most likely women, hid together, no doubt terrified, praying a little, guarding the door of the house. What did they expect? Trouble. Maybe a rebellion. Probably death. But then it happened. And happens. Who knew that God could come down upon us in being divided tongues like fire? When we ask with the people standing out there in all that fire and wind, "What does this thing mean?" we may intend a more literal translation, "What does this thing wish to be?" Who is God who appears to us in this way, and what does God wish by revealing Godself to us at this moment as being divided tongues like fire?

Maybe earlier, the people hanging around a living Jesus ask themselves similar questions. Then, the Jesus walking around the gospels, even though he speaks in parables much of the time, gives those who hear him a chance at understanding what they ought to be and do ("Listen to me; look on me and you will see God," "Here is what God wishes:"). In Acts, Jesus is gone. Without Jesus standing in front of us, how do we parse out Pentecost? "Being divided tongues of fire" equals . . . what the Holy Spirit is at the beginning of Acts. "Being divided," "tongues," "fire" each touches literal and figurative worlds of meaning, yet as we begin to think about them, we pull back. When we try to be on one or the other side of "being divided," "tongues," "fire," we are not sure where we are. This odd group of words Luke sets together can best be understood in context, by looking at what comes next, not by making the move into metaphor. We return to those people sitting in a house together. And we watch what happens.

The violence of the wind, fiery tongues settling down upon them, breaks up all the hiding and sitting. Being filled with the Holy Spirit, those gathered together begin speaking in multiple languages not their own, languages carefully listed in vv. 9–11. The sound of the Holy Spirit draws a crowd of people who among them speak all these languages. Two Greek words, *synelthen* and *synechythe*, describe what hearing their own languages does to the crowd; these same words might characterize the action of the Holy Spirit anywhere in Acts. Our translations, the crowd "came together," "gathered" and "was confused," "was bewildered," miss the repeated *syn* in the Greek, miss the verbal repetition that pushes these two actions toward one another. The Holy Spirit both gathers us up and confuses us. Things are not what we think they are. (And we didn't even see the being divided tongues.) Yet, if we listen to the Spirit, we hear our own language, our own in the midst of all sorts of other languages. Here, community, or the beginnings of it, is odd because it is not exactly shared vision; it is side by side understandings of what the Holy Spirit is saying, "the great things of God," all at the same time to each one of us, separately, while we are being gathered together.

What Acts Acts Out

What does this do for and to us? We generally understand the story of Pentecost to lead to the idyllic, "Everyone who believed were together and had things in common; they would sell their possessions and goods and distribute the proceeds to all, as any had need" (2:44–45). It does. But it also ends more immediately with members of the crowd sneering, calling those taken up by the being divided tongues of flame "drunkards." It ends with the quick greedy move that surfaces before you know it in utopian moments throughout history, with the story of Ananias and Sapphira, then with those who witness what happens to Ananias and Sapphira frightening and confusing followers of Peter and Paul. It ends with people who had been scared and hiding, getting up and travelling throughout the known world. It doesn't end. The Holy Spirit moves us through time and space to speak "the great things of God" another time, another place.

As Acts progresses, the "being divided tongues" perhaps burn out the chaff from the wheat; certainly "being divided tongues" picks up contiguous meaning. What is Acts if it is not the stories inherent in our "being divided tongues," our being Jews, Romans, Greeks, Barbarians, eunuchs, Pharisees, fishermen, deacons, preachers, gentile widows, slaves, magicians, centurions, idol makers . . . . The very lists of all the places Peter, Paul, Philip and the rest of the company go to, return to, see on the way emphasize how separate we are, how each of us is his or her own problem; each place requires its own message. Maybe in Malta, the cause/effect started by the snake and what it is next to, the wood pile Paul collects for the fire, acts out for us Acts. God puts you someplace. You try to build a fire (remember those tongues—exactly what sort of fire is Paul building?), and a snake breaks loose. Who would have expected this? Maybe we should; maybe this is one of Acts' lessons. We are in peculiar places. And we are invited, through the Holy Spirit, to bring the kingdom of heaven to these places.

In Acts, the Holy Spirit sends out the apostles to redeem the particulars. What we know in Acts is not so much that we Christians are in a body or a building, but that we are in a dangerous, glorious world that needs redemption. In fact, because of the facts we are in, it may be necessary for us not to be together. "Being divided tongues," a metonym which shows us the Holy Spirit, presses on us, describes us, and as it does, sends us out with our mission.

Paul's not being dead at the end of Acts respects the "deep structure" of Acts; he is still moving about. (I grappled with him just yesterday.) The work of Acts is not over. Living in our world is as simple and as difficult as living in the world of Paul, of Peter and Stephen and Philip and . . . . Wonders happen here, but not necessarily, as they seem to work themselves out, for any good purpose. As we stand alone looking out at what we see, we may feel paralyzed, unable to do anything but just to stay inside, consider our individual losses, stare at a snake. But Acts teaches us to inch forward or upward or sideways into what is next. Because our facts are part of a deep structure, one we cannot leap to, but one we can glimpse from time to time, one we can move toward.

— XXXI —

An Easter Story

I LOVE SHOPPING FOR Easter chocolate. For Henry, Alex, and David, of course. But Eric and Kristen with their daughters, Leila and Mia, Jason and Sarah with Ally Rose, Michael, Noah, and now Nicolas, along with David's mom, Don, Chris, really, all sorts of people come, celebrate with us, and this means loads and loads of chocolate, a giant Easter egg hunt, ham, brussel sprouts, salads, fresh bread, homemade macaroni and cheese, what else? Oh, and Pat's wonderful coconut bunny cake. Saturday night whoever is in town sits around my kitchen table and colors eggs. We leave them in cartons, then a bunny comes some time while we are asleep, exchanges the eggs for baskets filled with chocolate, and hides the eggs all over the yard for Sunday morning. Maybe there is no better candy than Easter chocolate. Caramel-filled eggs are my favorite, but chocolate lambs, chicks, bunnies, carrots, all of it works. Not to mention, the cascarones, light streaming through confetti, giggling, then full-blown laughing, and lots and lots of running here and there.

This past year, there was some talk of our going to a sunrise service, then, out at our farm, everyone started arriving. Big cousins lifting and twirling little cousins. The little cousins trailing behind Alex. Leila once told her father that she was going to marry Alex when she grew up. Eric was not sure that would work. Exasperated, Leila looked him right in the eye, "Who are you, the love police?" Indeed. To see Henry picking up Noah in order to check for eggs in trees, to see, for a split second, all that kindness spilling out of him, I want to stand and watch them forever. And then Alex cracks a cascarone on Henry's head. All out war. More confetti. More eggs. Finally lunch. Afterwards everyone does what he or she wants. I load up the truck with any little person who hopes to visit the horses. Alex and David hold Michael's and Noah's hands as they walk down to fish in the ponds. Even through the dusty truck window, I can see David's smile. All the girls come with me. Sam, our pony, is very obliging. He has never been brushed so much, maybe never looked so good.

But, at the end of the day, Alex seemed out of sorts. I thought he was sorry that most everyone was gone. We scrounged through chocolates, looking for ones with caramel. I was starting to tell Alex about Nicolas' baby steps and his chasing bubbles from the bubble wand. But Alex wasn't listening. Instead, he said, very quietly, as if it did not really matter to him, "We didn't go to church. We didn't hear the story." Hmmm. We had not. And, now that I thought about it, it was Alex who most wanted to go to the sunrise service. I found a bible. David, Henry, Don, and I sat and listened to Alex read the Easter story from Matthew. He reads so beautifully. All of it, the earthquake, the "then go quickly and tell his disciples he has been raised from the dead," the plotting priests and soldiers, the doubters and Jesus talking, happened right before us; it was late, but it was still Easter.

Late and still. The next month I graduated from seminary. Friends, family, so many people showed up for the ceremonies. Even my mother. I was not sure that she was going to come. Worse, I had the wrong time for the church service, so we walked in just after it had started. But there she and her husband were, sitting on a pew in the back. We all piled in around them. She seemed intent on following what was going on. As she watched first this speaker then that singer, I looked with her at everyone assembled behind the pulpit. Most of my teachers were there. I could hear some of their individual voices in the singing. Bill Greenway, taller than everyone next to him, boomed out part of a hymn. That voice, its strength and insistence, is Bill's secret weapon. One day, he

An Easter Story

cornered an entire class into the proposition that following Christ should lead to our forgiving even Hitler. I slipped out. (Whatever they thought, I wasn't going to forgive Hitler. It was not my business to.) When I turned from Bill back to my mother, I lost my bearing. All these kind, well-meaning people, what was I doing among them? We were all supposed to be singing, but I had picked up the wrong book.

A faulty overhead light made Bill's face shine too much. His colors did not stay put. And then I remembered the bubbles at Easter. Nicolas had been crying. The other children were nowhere to be found. So I picked him up. We went into the front yard and blew and shook and waved bubbles. Squealing and laughing, he stumbled after them. I sat down in the grass. Chasing bubbles, Nicolas used my shoulders, my head, my hair to make his way toward them. I lay down in the grass and watched with Nicolas one giant bubble form, then float upwards. The light streaming through started sea-green, then pink, then purple dancing about the bubble's surface. We could not take our eyes away from it. We were both so happy. I don't remember the bubble's bursting. My mother was trying hard to keep up with the pages of the hymnal. Bill's colors, the church's peculiar lighting, bled into her. Watching my mother now in the shadows, now present, flipping back and forth, adjusting her glasses, I realized that somehow I had forgiven her. Light just barely glancing off the surface sets color in motion. We can't help it. It is too beautiful.

Three more weeks and we were in France. Our phones told us how far we walked as we ate our way through Paris. On one of our days in the Louvre, we walked seventeen miles, eight or nine of them inside. Because I love England, I had been a little skeptical about our trip. It turns out I also love France. History everywhere so obvious that you touch it, walk through it, consider again and again what it might mean. Alex and I looked down from a castle that Richard the Lionheart had commandeered. We saw the river below, thought about battles after battles seven times in a hundred years as one side was France then England then France . . . . And of the work. Building and rebuilding impossibly thick rock walls.

People hiding in caves from the Vikings who brought their boats down the river. Monuments marking plague villages. Crusaders' graves (Alex discovered these behind the cathedral in Sarlat. He recognized the Templar's Cross). In all of it, over and over, we found ourselves among the shadows of people who had tried very hard to orient themselves. Carving perfect runes in the rocks. Designing those monuments. Marking that the dead had been part of the journey there and back again. Being healed only to die. Dying only to . . . .

Not a circle, but steps. At Gouffre de Padirac, we went down hundreds of them lining the wall of a deep, deep moss and fern-filled hole, ending at a tiny elevator that took us down even farther. At the bottom, inside and under the small mountain we had climbed an hour before, we found a river waiting for us. A boatman ushered us onto a flat boat (of course, you know what we were thinking about), and we floated the river. Cave lights opened up the stalactites, stalagmites, chandeliers all around. Our guide was kind enough to make jokes in broken English. If we had not heard them, we might have lost our bearing. That overwhelming beauty, the river streaming through then later out of the mountain, carrying with it tiny pieces of crystal that lay embedded in the landscape, ready to pop, what we were seeing, it was too much. Underground water, the paths it creates, the residue it leaves behind that, year after year, becomes more and more unimaginably beautiful, growing up and down out of the rock, wait for a bit of light to show themselves to anyone who happens by.

Maybe that is what glory is. Or what glory means. In Lewie's classes, we could never quite pin down glory and all the Greek verbs connected to it. The twinkle in Lewie's eyes hinted that we were almost there. But then Lewie, perhaps the finest teacher I have ever had, would shrug as he smiled, "You know, I don't exactly know the answer. But if they ask you at the pearly gates, you might guess." Lewie gave the sermon at graduation. He spoke about God's love pulling us forward, about God's love seeping into time, into our stories, calling us all. To believe in the possibility of every tear's being dried. To believe in the coming and becoming

An Easter Story

kingdom. To hope and watch and do what you can. This is what I want. This is Easter for me.

In the meantime, in the middle of the Ile de la Cite, we were headed toward Notre Dame, expecting to be appropriately impressed. Henry asked us to change course. "We need to go to Sainte-Chapelle first. Notre Dame is fine, but we'll want plenty of time at Sainte-Chapelle." The whole of the week we made our way through Paris Henry guided us. He had been there before and had taken it all in. His instincts so far had been exactly right. By memory, he led us to an intersection where we found signs that brought us to tall gates and armed police officers in front of an ancient compound. Sainte-Chapelle at first appears to be, and I think at different points in time has been, part of police work, a prison even. We walked through a corridor that looked like something in a VA hospital then through a metal detector into a courtyard. Low clouds hung over us. The outside of the chapel was gray, grim, without gardens, without landscape, Gothically pointed but more goth than Gothic. Somewhat confused, we went into the wrong doors and ended up in the gift shop. At the near end was a worn staircase which spiraled into darkness. Its breadth allowed only one person at a time. The thought of a group of people coming down when we were half way up made me hesitate. I heard voices above and hurried so that I lost my breath. At the top of the stairs, I came out into what I thought was a small room. It was still darkish. I wished we had gone to Notre Dame.

A little dizzy, I began to look for Henry, Alex, and David. Not paying attention to what was around me, I saw Alex and walked as fast as I could toward him. He was standing in the middle of what turned out to be the sanctuary. He did not see me because he was looking up. His body was still; his mouth, slightly open; his eyes, opened wide. I glanced up, then I stopped to see what I was seeing. Light filled with color everywhere, thousands of stories told one at a time and all at once in panes of glass. Everywhere. Color and light. Patterns with small stories making larger stories. A man in a robe laying down globes and flowers. Knights fighting. Bones and creatures with wings. Books being carried. Sheep being tended.

People sick and dying. People being baptized. Children dancing. The cross. Right to left or left to right? Or down to up? Alex, then Henry, came and stood next to me. We found a place to sit. And we just looked and looked and looked. And prayed together. And thought about all those people in the courtyard over maybe centuries working on glass and breaking it and keeping it in order with what tools, what fires; where did the sand for the glass come from? How did they travel with glass? How did all this work? How could it be? And yet it was. In the middle of the mess of history, the mess of life, we sat together and tried to take in all those stories worked in love, working with light toward a whole story, a kind of perfection, bearing witness to a perfecting love that works in shards of glass.

www.ingramcontent.com/pod-product-compliance
Lightning Source LLC
Chambersburg PA
CBHW070914160426
43193CB00011B/1455